CRIMINAL JUSTICE
PLANNING AND DEVELOPMENT

Volume 4
SAGE RESEARCH PROGRESS SERIES IN CRIMINOLOGY

ABOUT THIS SERIES

The *Sage Research Progress Series in Criminology* is intended for those professionals and students in the fields of criminology, criminal justice, and law who are interested in the nature of current research in their fields. Each volume in the series—four to six new titles will be published in each calendar year—focuses on a theme of current and enduring concern; and each volume contains a selection of previously unpublished essays . . . drawing upon presentations made at the previous year's Annual Meeting of the American Society of Criminology.

The *Series* begins in 1977 with four volumes, selected from papers delivered at the 28th Annual Meeting of the American Society of Criminology held in Tucson, Arizona, on November 4-7, 1976. The volumes in this inaugural year include:

- *Theory in Criminology: Contemporary Views,*
  edited by Robert F. Meier
- *Juvenile Delinquency: Little Brother Grows Up,*
  edited by Theodore N. Ferdinand
- *Contemporary Corrections: Social Control and Conflict,*
  edited by C. Ronald Huff
- *Criminal Justice Planning and Development,*
  edited by Alvin W. Cohn

We are pleased that these initial volumes in the *Sage Research Progress Series in Criminology* so well represent significant interdisciplinary contributions to the literature on criminology, juvenile delinquency, criminal justice administration, legal and ethical issues, and related areas. Comments and suggestions from our readers will be welcomed.

SERIES EDITORS:

James A. Inciardi
University of Delaware
Newark, Delaware

Gilbert Geis
University of California
Irvine, California

June 1977

SAGE RESEARCH PROGRESS SERIES IN CRIMINOLOGY
VOLUME 4

CRIMINAL JUSTICE PLANNING and DEVELOPMENT

Edited by
Alvin W. Cohn

Published in cooperation with the
AMERICAN SOCIETY of CRIMINOLOGY

SAGE Publications Beverly Hills London

For information address:

SAGE PUBLICATIONS, INC.
275 South Beverly Drive
Beverly Hills, California 90212

SAGE PUBLICATIONS LTD
28 Banner Street
London EC1Y 8QE

Printed in the United States of America

International Standard Book Number 0-8039-0918-7 (cloth)
International Standard Book Number 0-8039-0913-6 (paper)

Library of Congress Catalog Card No. 77-81154

FIRST PRINTING

CONTENTS

for

Herbert, Sara, and Charlotte Slovis

Alvin W. Cohn
University Research Corporation

INTRODUCTION

For the past quarter of a century, space age technology has had significant influence on our culture. The use of computers and all of the software associated with automatic processing has spawned a new generation of management specialists. Whether one is classical, human relations, or functionalist in orientation, the impact of this new technology is inescapable.

One noted social scientist, Robert Boguslaw, refers to such managers as "social engineers" and suggests that they may even be "new utopians." In fact, he states:

> Utopia is a place that seems to belong either to the past or to the future, and we tend to think of utopians as being either starry-eyed philosophers or wild-eyed reformers. But there is a new breed of utopians afoot . . . These are the people who are known by such titles as systems engineer, computer manufacturer, operations researcher, computer programmer, data processing specialist, or, more simply, system designer . . . [and] Most of the new utopians would be either amused or shocked at being called "social engineers." [Boguslaw, 1965: 1]

The administration of criminal justice is not immune from the demands and processes of these social engineers.

In an age when bureaucracy recognizes the value of scarce resources and attempts to reallocate such more effectively and efficiently, it is the systems analyst who plays a large role. The dilemma facing him, however, is that in attempting to produce meaningful results, goals must be explicit and actual systems well defined.

In criminal justice, neither of these is known. Further, the process for clarifying goals and systems is not being resolved by practitioners or theoreticians. The result is muddy water and the likelihood of making it clear is problematic. Following the work of Freed (1969), Cohn (1974) has commented on the nonsystem aspects of criminal justice. He summarizes some of the recent literature, pointing out that most writers and researchers have indicated that the network of criminal justice services is as much fragmented, splintered, and divided as it has ever been.

Planning and developing criminal justice services and programs demands a systemic effort. Buckley's definition of a system is a helpful starting point in our efforts to understand what is required:

> . . . (a) system . . . may be described generally as a complex of elements or components directly or indirectly related in a causal network, such that each component is related to at least some others in a more or less stable way within any particular period of time . . . The particular kinds of more or less stable interrelationships of components that become established at any time constitute the particular structure of the system at that time, thus achieving a kind of "whole" with some degree of continuity and boundary. [Buckley, 1967: 41]

Police, courts, and corrections, the usual categories within criminal justice, not only have been unable to define missions for their own agencies, but there has been little accomplished in terms of defining a total system or set of accepted interrelationships. Each, obviously, is concerned with the reduction and control of crime. Each makes demands upon the others. But there is probably more role ambiguity and goal misunderstanding than should be tolerated at this stage in our development of social engineering.

As we explore this total systems view, we can see in very sharp relief the many roles played by significant actors and the variety of functions served by their host agencies. Analyses also illuminate the serious conflicts experienced by those actors and agencies as they interact with one another. We continually hear such epithets as "the courts are handcuffing the police"; "punishment mitigates against rehabilitation"; "the police are inept in dealing with victims and witnesses"; and "correctional programs are ineffective in reducing crime on the streets." O'Leary and Ryan, in commenting on the nonsystem state of affairs and the concomitant conflict in criminal justice, stated:

> Rarely are conflicts openly explored; even more rarely are they handled successfully. The notion that criminal justice is a system whose parts must effectively articulate is more often employed as a pious aspiration than as something to be applied seriously. [1969: 2]

The existence of conflict should not be viewed as unhealthy necessarily. In fact, just the opposite, theoretically, is true. Lipset maintains that the very existence of a stable democracy requires conflict and is the foundation upon which our government was founded—with the creation of co-equal branches of government:

> Clevage—where it is legitimate—contributes to the integration of societies and organizations . . . consensus on the norms of tolerance which a society or organization accepts has often developed only as a result of basic conflict, and requires the continuance of conflict to sustain it. [1963:1]

From this perspective, as O'Leary and Ryan maintain, conflict is seen as necessary to growth and constructive transactions among people and organizations. "Thus, the goal should not be to try to eliminate all conflict within the criminal justice system, but that which is clearly and importantly dysfunctional" (1969: 3).

The above presupposes that the development of a true system within criminal justice is a desirable goal. While the merits of such a position may be obvious and even have been extolled, it is possible that the development of such a system may itself be dysfunctional insofar as our kind of government is concerned. This is especially important when we consider the nature of our "check and balance" system. That is, no branch of government is supposed to have grater power or control over another branch. Theoretically, this is true. Pragmatically, it may not be as true as we would like. For example, some maintain that the courts have assumed too much control and power and have begun to intervene in administrative affairs of the other branches of government.

That the courts have been forced to intervene in such matters as prison discipline, arrest procedures, and defendant rights is viewed by some as indeed a check and balance system at work. For others, these interventions are percieved as meddling. Who is right is irrelevant in terms of our discourse at the moment. What is important is that the actions of one form of government frequently impinge upon others, and this can produce a level of conflict which precludes the development of effective interpersonal and interagency relationships.

From another point of view, some argue that the development of a true system is operationally inadvisable. That is, it is not practical to build unity among the criminal justice network of services for each set of programs has a radically different mission from the others. The police are supposed to apprehend offenders; the courts are supposed to process them; and corrections is assigned the responsibility of watching over those who are convicted and, according to some, rehabilitate them. These missions, some claim, are inherently oppositional and cannot—and should not— be merged into a unified system. Furthermore, if a true system is developed, one agency or set of services is likely to achieve superiority over another, which inevitably would lead to greater conflict and less meaningful programs for communities and clients.

Notwithstanding the arguments posed above, each agency and service within criminal justice probably could benefit from better planning, more coordination, and additional consideration of needs and problems of others. Moreover, the involvement of community groups in policy setting and implementation should be encouraged if for no other reason than a democratic state demands such involvement. The people have a right to speak and government officials have an obligation to listen. Together, a mandate to do something about the crime problem could be enunciated and put into practice. Such a liaison is more likely to bring about meaningful reform, which few deny is needed.

For the past decade, the Law Enforcement Assistance Administration (LEAA) has been charged with the responsibility of assisting states in the development and implementation of responsible and comprehensive planning in criminal justice administration at the state level of government. Although there have been some improvements in services, critics of the block grant approach utilized by LEAA maintain that the Safe Streets Act program has failed, especially since LEAA never developed an aggresive leadership role. The Advisory Commission on Intergovernment Relations (ACIR) in assessing the achievements and failures of the legislation and LEAA, stated:

> It is clear that the program has had a history of controversy. Billed as a new administrative approach, the act was neither legislated nor administered as a pure block grant. Its goals have been overwhelmingly ambitious, to a degree that appears with hindsight to be naive. These goals (of reducing crime and impacting crime rates) are yet to be fulfilled. [1977: 47]

An ideal planning process requires not only the explication of organizational (if not systemic) goals, but a set of goals which can be translated into an action strategy to be implemented by all incumbents of the organization, regardless of hierarchical rank. But criminal justice managers, according to Cohn, (1973), generally have not been trained in management principles or procedures, which mitigates aginst such effective planning. For the most part, they learn how to run their organizations through trial and error, through experience, and through the dictates and pressures by others in positions of management, especially elected superiors.

Because of their naivete, they often think that planning is merely a process of delineating what programs they would like to have, without first having conducted a responsible needs assessment. Planning is not words, communications, or public relations. It is not merely the setting down on paper what is desirable. Instead, it should be viewed as a rigorous process that demonstrates a responsiveness to needs, an awareness of resources, and an honest approach to matching needs with resources in a manner that is likely to produce significant results—results which, if measured, will answer the question of the extent to which goals are being met.

Criminal justice managers generally do not appreciate the difference between organizational achievements and institutional success as Selznick (1957: 27) uses the terms. The former is used to depict the many activities of an organization, such as training events, research activities, and numbers of clients being served. Not any of these nor all of these collectively necessarily add up to the accomplishment of organizational goals. Institutional success, on the other hand, is accomplished only when the organization's explicit goals are indeed met.

However, goals are set within an organization, they must be developed in an achievable way. It is only then that effective plans can be developed to implement them. In the end result, a plan becomes nothing more than a blueprint for managers and subordinates alike, working in concert, to accomplish some given objectives. Although writing for the corporate and business world, Ewing offers a definition of planning that is apt:

> . . . (planning is) a method of guiding managers so that their decisions and actions affect the future of the organization in a consistent and rationale manner, and in a way desired by top management. [1968: 17-18]

Ewing goes on to state that "desired by top management" is of great significance for it is a phrase which implies goal setting. "It implies a conscious management effort to look at itself and its environment and, on the basis of facts and aspirations, make the best choice possible in the range of alternatives. (1968: 19).

We have previously suggested that conflict can be viewed as healthy for an organization as it strives to harness the invevitability of change and avoid its dysfunctional aspects. Mary Parker Follett, a keen observer of administrative practice once said: "When we think that we have *solved* a problem, well, by the very process of solving, new elements or forces come into the situation and you have a new problem on your hands to be solved" (1937: 166). Thus, as we examine the effects of LEAA on the development of comprehensive planning in criminal justice administration and the efforts of the various State Planning Agencies as well, we are confronted with a dilemma: the innovations instituted to solve one problem often create others because effectiveness in an organization depends on many different factors, some of which are incompatible with others.

The very improvements in some conditions that further the achievements of an organization's objectives often interfere with other conditions within the organization as well as in other organizations. As the police develop new technologies in communications, for example, this not only alters patterns of interpersonal relations and communications between hierarchies of personnel, it impacts on its relationships with citizens and other organizations with which they are in daily and routine contact.

If the police increase their effectiveness in apprehending offenders, this has impact on court dockets and eventually on correctional caseloads. Thus, there are dilemmas at every turn on the crossroad, and these dilemmas are not easily resolved wihout producing new and different levels of conflict which also need to be resolved.

Hopefully, as Blau and Scott point out:

> New problems are internally generated in organizations in the process of solving old ones. However, the experience gained in solving earlier problems is not lost but contributes to the search for solutions to later problems. These facts suggest that the process of organizational development is dialectical—problems appear, and while the process of solving them tends to give rise to new problems, learning has occurred which influences how the new challenges are met. [1962: 250-251]

The administration of criminal justice services in the United States currently is undergoing considerable change. But this is not much different from the view earlier writers must have taken. Today, however, there is change with a new self-conscious dimension, namely, *direction;* and this is the nitty gritty of *development.* As Meadows (1971: 294) indicates, "Goals and measures and tempos and urgencies have been added to the sense of change everywhere." Thus, the winds of change are blowing in some well-sensed direction and, one hopes, practitioners and academicians in the field of criminal justice are at least feeling the breeze.

Many people are questioning the direction of this wind and whether or not it is promising a brave or even a new world. Some portend a "future shock." Others believe that the change process is much too slow and not in the best interests of selected populations. They demand radicalization. Still others believe that change is occuring too rapidly and not in a positive direction. They ask for a slow down; a time for reflection; an opportunity to regroup. Thus, even those who are concerned with change are in conflict, not only in terms of substance, but with regard to the very process itself.

The great learning, however, may not lie in designing appropriate change mechanisms. It may be, as a famous social psychologist, Kurt Lewin, once wrote, that a social organism becomes understandable only *after* one attempts to change it. It often happens, therefore, that management's awareness for a new organization design emerges only after the start of an intensive change process. And even were it possible for a manager to be omniscient in developing a master blueprint before introducing any organizational change, it is doubtful that his colleagues or his subordinates would readily accept the new design or have the required skills for making it work. For these reasons, managers need to be as skillful at handling the question of *how* to introduce change as they are in diagnosing *what* needs to be changed.

Finally, while managers must perceive themselves as change agents and develop change strategies in goal directed ways, they must also recognize the inherent relationship between change and social policy. Developing goals, however explicit and meaningful they may be, is insufficient. These goals and the processes needed to implement them must be placed in proper context. This context can appropriately be defined as a social policy which explains why a certain goal is appropriate for the organization at a given time and place. A social policy is needed to assist the manager in understanding the social environment in which his organization operates.

Insofar as criminal justice is concerned, clear and distinct social policies are needed to understand what is expected of its various agencies and actors. A police chief, as well as a correctional administrator or a presiding judge, must appreciate "community" demands. What values, what philosophies, what needs—and from what groups, are all aspects of social policy development. Thus, not to know or to know and to be insensitive to an external environment is to perpetuate the isolation of criminal justice agencies many administrators have lamented for decades. To involve the community (however it is defined) is, of course, a difficult task, for it slows down movement and development in the short term. Yet, as many have noted, in the long term, greater coordination, improved communications, and consensus over direction and goals are quite likely to improve the state of the art in criminal justice administration.

The papers which follow in this volume comment on several aspects of the material presented above. They do not fit precisely into any schema about planning, change, goal setting, development, or criminal justice management. However, they are concerned with several of the significant actors and agencies in the criminal justice network of services for which sound planning and development are essential.

The first two articles discuss planning and goal setting. In "Criminal Justice Planning: Prediction or Projection," Michael S. Katz looks at the planning process in considerable detail and points out the responsibility of criminal justice planners in defining mission. Additionally, he illustrates both the difference and relationship between policy planning and program planning. He urges that planning for crime prevention be based on the knowledge that crime and behavior cannot be separated. Finally, he argues for long-range planning which involves the general citizenry.

Ronald Schneider and Richard Foster, in "Planning and Decentralization: Can the Criminal Justice System Accommodate both Demands," continue some of the dialogue of Katz with regard to the nonsystem aspects of criminal justice, particularly pointing out that subsystem changes are not usually taken into consideration in policy formulation. They suggest that the general public's antipathy toward centralization appears to present a major obstacle to comprehensive, systemic planning in criminal justice administration. He urges the development of specific goals so that performance measures can be utilized to calculate the success—or failure—of organizational objectives.

Marlynn L. May's paper, "Education for Careers in Criminal Justice: A Challenge to Liberal Arts," examines the problems associated with producing competent and employable personnel for criminal justice agencies. Particularly, the author reports on a study which explored the relationship between liberal arts education (especially in sociology) and criminal justice careers. He concludes that a liberal arts education is preferred over others by those who do the hiring because such graduates tend to have breadth of knowledge and skills in writing, oral expression, and critical analysis.

In the next paper, "Toward a Rational Resolution of Ethical Dilemmas in the Criminal Justice System," Robert H. Aronson examines the role of the attorney and his or her education insofar as professional responsibility and ethics development are concerned. He maintains that until a fundamental disagreement concerning the proper functioning of attorneys under the Adversary System is resolved, the hoped-for confidence in their ethical conduct is not likely to change. He asks practicing attorneys to play an active role in defining their responsibilities and, further, he advocates a System Model with regard to professionalism and ethical behavior.

"Studying discrepancies between Police-Citizen Anomia Levels," by Robert M. Regoli, is a paper which examines the consequences of interactions between two other significant and highly visible actors in the network of criminal justice services: police and citizens. From a planning perspective, the author hypothesizes that it will be important to neutralize the "occupational demands" of police before their attitudes and value patterns will be similar to those of citizens. Further, he explores the lower level of anomia among police, as compared to sampled citizens. Based on "radical" criminology tenets, he suggests that since police become part of the "ruling elite," they become insulated against anomia producing conditions.

Sentencing offenders has received considerable research attention in recent years, especially since judges and critics alike have expressed concerns over the issue of disparities. With the relatively recent advent of sentencing institutes and sentencing guidelines, together with proposals for the abolition of parole and the establishment of fixed or flat sentences (presumtive sentencing), planning for change in the courts—particularly judicial decision-making—is receiving new impetus. Carol Bohmer, in "Psychiatrists and Presentence Reports: A Case of Role Stress," looks at the processes by which judges receive formal advice, especially the role of the psychiatric presentence report. Additionally, she explores psychiatrists' perceptions of the services they provide the court and the problems of such work, including role conflicts and role ambiguities. Finally, there is some discussion about the role in this process of another significant actor in the criminal justice process, the defendant and his or her rights prior to sentencing.

Another area which has been receiving widespread interest lately is that of diversion. Seen by some as a panacea and by others as a palliative, diversion, nonetheless, is a process which keeps some offenders from entering the criminal justice network and helps others to be released from its clutches. The last two papers deal with this subject, but from different points of view. In "Criminal Justice Diversion for Whom," Duane C. McBride and Susan G. Dalton explore diversion as a successful alternative to incarceration. In a study of an actual program, they examine applicable offenses for such an alternative and analyze the characteristics of a sampled population which accepted diversion. The authors conclude that diversion requires considerable planning, especially since unanticipated consequences can affect successful programming.

"Diversion and the Justice System: Evaluating the Results," by Arnold Binder, concludes the volume with a report on the process of evaluation in criminal justice, particularly focusing on diversion. He discusses the divergence in opinion regarding the effectiveness of such programs and shares three reasons for the current state of affairs. They include problems of definition, conceptualization, and the biases and needs of evaluators. He concludes with advice for all who are—or should be— concerned with planning and development in criminal justice: "We must know the 'what works,' the 'for whom,' and 'the optimum conditions',"

—Alvin W. Cohn, editor

REFERENCES

Advisory Commission on Intergovernmental Relations [ACIR] (1977). Safe streets reconsidered: The block grant experience 1968-1975. Washington, D.C.: U.S. Government Printing Office.

BLAU, P.M. and SCOTT, W.R. (1962). Formal organizations. San Francisco: Chandler.

BOGUSLAW, R. (1965). The new utopians: A study of system design and social change. Englewood Cliffs, N.J.: Prentice-Hall.

BUCKLEY, W. (1967). Sociology and modern systems theory. Englewood Cliffs, N.J.: Prentice-Hall.

COHN, A.W. (1973). "The failure of correctional management." Crime & Delinquency (July).

——— (1974). "Training in the criminal justice nonsystem." Federal Probation (June).

EWING, D.W. (1968). The practice of planning. New York: Harper and Row.

FOLLETT, M.P. (1937). "The process of control." In L. Gulick and L. Urwick (eds.), Papers on the science of administration. New York: Institute of Public Administration.

FREED, D.J. (1969). "The nonsystem of criminal justice." In J.S. Campbell, J.R. Sahid, and D.P. Stang (eds.), Law and order reconsidered: A staff report to the national commission on the causes and prevention of violence. Washington, D.C.: U.S. Government Printing Office.

LIPSET, S.M. (1963). Political man, the social bases of politics. Garden City, N.Y.: Anchor Books.

MEADOWS, P. (1971). The many faces of change: Explorations in the theory of social change. Cambridge, Mass: Schenkman.

O'LEARY, V. and RYAN, E. (1969). A study of conflict resolution in criminal justice. New York: National Council on Crime and Delinquency.

SELZNICK, P. (1957). Leadership in administration: A sociological interpretation. New York: Harper and Row.

Michael S. Katz
Criminal Justice Planning Committee of Washoe County, Nevada

1

CRIMINAL JUSTICE PLANNING: Prediction or Projection

Planning is the process of preparing a set of decisions for action in the future, directed at achieving goals by optimum means." This definition by Dror (1968) provides us with a generalized statement of intent of the reason for doing planning. But planning as a task to be accomplished versus planning to obtain results must be separated and identified.

All too often we engage in a "planning" activity as a means to an end, the end result being the award of a sum of federal grant-in-aid monies. While the end in itself is not necessarily improper, the methods used may very well be. This is a situation that requires a closer look at past performance and current "state of the art" if we are to develop criminal justice planning to a higher degree of professionalism and responsiblity.

Planning has been identified by many different philosophies, methodologies, and descriptions of technical manipulation. It has been viewed as both a savior and a nemesis. It has been severely criticized and complimented, but the ultimate evaluation is going to have to lie in the answer to the question: "Does it work?"

The criminal justice system is not unlike large corporations when it comes to the problems of planning. The system is large, multifaceted, and very decentralized.

But it has one important feature that must never be forgotten: it deals with and controls human behavior. Unlike planning for corporate production goals or a large investment portfolio, the criminal justice system deals with the lives and futures of people. Thus, caution must be exercised when "planning," since the goals that are being set have profound and lasting implications on the lives of many, many people. We are continually refining the criminal justice planning process to be more responsive to the system's problems, but in that process of refinement, there must be an improvement upon the social situations which make it worth the cost of producing those refinements.

Within this paper, I will not discuss the technical methods of carrying-out the planning function; these are covered in many fine publications. What I do feel is important is the need for criminal justice planners to establish a definition of their mission. One big area that I believe needs conceptual clarification is the issue of *policy planning* versus *program planning.* Each has its place, but policy planning must be a prerequisite to any thought about program planning. Too often a program is developed that will hopefully influence future policy decisions. I do not think we can afford the luxury of "experimenting" with programs to see if one will work or not; we are dealing with people, not stocks or machines.

As a precursor to the planning process, we *must* begin to pay more attention to the area of evaluation research. "Evaluation research is defined as the application of scientific principles, methods, and theories to identify, describe, conceptualize, measure, predict, change and control those factors or variables important to the development of effective human service delivery systems" (Struening, 1975). The importance of this field lies in its underlying role, which is generally directed at determining what is most effective, valuable, desirable, or useful, rather than a determination of supporting a hypothesis. The demonstration of relative value is the key benefit.

Because our level of knowledge regarding the intricacies of human behavior and motivation is limited, fragmented, and inconclusive, we need to look at many levels of evaluation research to strengthen our knowledge. We also need to look beyond the agencies of the criminal justice system to the community as a whole when doing our planning.

As I have just indicated, an underlying problem is in the lack of definition about the mission of criminal justice planning. I do not mean to infer that planners do not know what they are doing, however, I am suggesting that there has never been a consensus upon the goal, i.e., do we attempt to predict what is going to happen or do we attempt to project what is going to happen.

Prediction, by definition, is a telling beforehand of an **occurrence that is going to happen, that is, a *prophecy*.** Projection on the other hand, can be defined as the treatment of what is essentially a subjective item as an objective and external item. Given the acceptance of those definitions, I find it extremely difficult to deal with a predictive model. I therefore suggest that criminal justice planning establish as its working format a model of projection; that is, taking the knowns and extending them out to a logical, and if need be, mathematical summation of past history. This is where the emphasis on the evaluation of programs and past methodologies will be of importance.

I recognize that projection has its pitfalls insofar as the hesitancy of many to base future results upon past actions is concerned. However, in support, I feel that the reams of existing research, particularly in the fields of the behavioral sciences, environmental sciences, computer sciences, and the like is the logical backbone for the baseline data that need to be developed and then added to by crime statistics, prosecution, and court information, as well as correctional information.

The conventional criminological approach to the question of finding the causes of crime has been to determine the extent to which delinquency is correlated with the number of individual and environmental factors that have produced a large number of statistical studies. This approach has been mainly concerned with the number of criminals caught after a series of conflicts between the criminal and society. Very little, if any, attention has been paid so far to the structure or nature of their conflicts or to the strategic and tactical considerations.

Many of the studies of past forecasting methods have concluded that a signifiicant cause of error is the underestimation or complete omission of certain factors in the environment which could have an impact upon the technology being forecasted. That is, the planner takes a narrow look at only the problem he is trying to forecast and as a result his forecast may be rendered invalid by some factor or factors which he has either ignored completely or whose impact he has grossly underestimated. A description of causality can be stated by saying that causal relations are the subclass of associations that meet several qualifying tests or conditions. Therefore, the job of the definition is to establish appropriate tests, which are the conditions of a relationship that must be met to be considered causal.

As Downey and Hunt have suggested, the geographic approach to crime must, ideally, synthesize ecological and physiological variables. Therefore, we must increase our ability to deal with complex issues that will enable us to identify a larger number of decision processes, situations, personality factors, and many, many more of the elements of any crime that need to be considered, without the pitfalls of simplification which characterizes our present tactics.

Statistics and data, as previously mentioned, are critical. They are the base upon which we must build our body of knowledge so that projection becomes as closely related to the real world as possible. Therefore, to establish position at any given time, to determine priorities for systematic change, and to assess the effects of any change, criminal justice agencies must develop reliable record systems and data analysis procedures that are appropriate to each type of agency. They must also lend themselves to comprehensive analysis among the various agencies, thus permitting assessment of the state of the system "as a whole." Once there is a clear definition of the functions to be performed, there must a selection of one or more parameters which would provide the quantitative descriptions. The selection of these parameters should be governed by the following considerations: (1) the parameter should be operational, (2) the parameter must be a true representation of the art, (3) the parameter must apply to diverse technical approaches performing the same functions, (4) the necessary historical data must be available, and (5) the data are consistent.

One needs to keep in mind the broad conception and operation of the criminal justice system. What is required to measure a level of functioning is a series of indexes reflecting the major decision-making points occurring within the system. We refer to these indexes as "system rates." The following chart shows the relations between system rates and rate determinants.

System Rates	*Rate State Determinants*
(1) Community Absorption	(1) Deviant behavior definitions
(2) Apprehension	(2) Deviant behavior levels
(3) Processing	(3) Community Resources
(4) Release	(4) Community Attitudes
(5) Reabsorption	(5) System philosophies
(6) Recidivision	(6) System efficiencies
	(7) Community-System coordination

The above mentioned system rates and rate determinants (Klein et al., 1971) is just one method by which we can get closer to looking at the totality of measurement within the criminal justice system. Another method is the tracing of cohort trails. The significance of tracing cohorts of offenders throughout the system and establishing the aforementioned system rates, is the possibility of evaluating the effects of alternative decisions that have been or could be made. This provides an extremely practical basis for developing a comprehensive criminal justice plan.

"Partly from lack of research, the system has moved without any sense of direction, without testing its assumptions or establishing priorities. Tradition, convenience or fashion have too often been substituted for analysis. Since less than one percent of the monies in Criminal Justice has been spent on research, it is not surprising that relatively little work has been done to develop the best ways to deter crime, and how to detect, apprehend, and rehabilitate criminals" (Thompson, 1972: 23-29).

No matter what theory and philosophy are used, methods of rational analysis must serve to provide precise calculation of the cost and returns to be expected for each feasible course of action and they must also be of benefit in determining whether a given course of action is feasible or not. Therefore, the decision maker must note the course of action open to him, the costs of each, and the returns of each because the "goodness" of a decision bears a strong relationship to the quality and completeness of the information upon which that decision is based. The whole purpose of rational analysis is to eliminate the need for handling on an intuitive basis those pieces of information which can be handled rationally and explicitly.

"Crime is normal because a society exempt from it is utterly impossible." Durkheim's (1964:67) classic formulation provides us with a timeless sense of perspective in contemplating the meaning and pervasiveness of crime and deviance in the human situation. Durkheim's analysis is confirmed, *interelia,* by compelling historic evidence and should therefore not surprise us that most, if not all, of us have violated legal norms on more than one occasion without being labeled or officially adjudictated as delinquents or criminals. "There is . . . no phenomenon that presents more indisputably all the systems of normality (than crime), since it appears closely connected with the conditions of all collective life. To make of crime a form of social morbidity would be to admit that morbidity is not something accidental, but, on the contrary, that in certain cases it grows out of the fundamental constitution of the living organism; it would result in wiping out all distinction between the physiological and the pathological. No doubt it is possible that crime itself will have abnormal form, as, for example, when its rate is unusually high. This excess is indeed undoubtedly morbid in nature. What is normal, simply, is the existence of criminality, provdided that it obtains and does not exceed, for each social type, a certain level, which is perhaps not impossible to fix" (Durkheim, 1950:60).

It is vital to recognize that criminal activity is a human activity. While crime is only one manifestation of human failings, it is a particularly important activity to study because of the nearly universalistic feeling that these acts can be controlled, moderated, reduced, or contained by public measures. It is this concept of control by public measure of the private act that needs to be studied. We must ask the question: what are the consequences to the person from the exterior contingencies placed upon him? In the view of Skinner (1971), "It is now clear that we must take into account what the environment does to an organism not only before but after it responds. Behavior is shaped and maintained by its consequences. Once we recognize this fact we can formulate the interaction between organism and environment in a much more comprehensive way."

In our planning attempts we quite often overlook the problem of resulting behavior as a goal toward which we should be striving. That is, a separation of crime and behavior is not possible; therefore, when we deal with crime prevention or crime deterrence activities we must base it upon the knowledge that these criminal activities are manifestations of human behavior. This was very well stated by George Vold (1958) when he said: "Crime always involves human behavior (acts) and the judgment or definitions (laws, customs, mores) of fellow human beings as to whether specific human behavior is appropriate and permissible, or is improper and forbidden. Crime and criminality lie in the area of behavior that is considered improper and forbidden. There is, therefore, always a dual problem of explanation—that of accounting for the definitions by which specific behavior comes to be considered as crime."

An explanation of criminal behavior is going to depend upon an explanation of behavior. Such an explanation necessarily involves many nonsociological factors. It is to be questioned at this time whether the sociologists have to be so concerned with human motivation. It seems to the writer that sociologists would do better to be more concerned with group reactions to certain types of behavior. The study of social structures is sociological; the study of human motivation is only quasi-sociological. A study of social systems in relation to the topic "Law and Society would eventually lead to a theory of crime" (Jeffery, 1956:672).

Any analytical description of a society or actions within that society may be couched in static terms, but the critical caution here is that social phenomena are in a constant state of flux and thus these analytical descriptions must be constantly revised. For example, within an economic framework of analysis, increases in the probability or severity of punishment should serve to deter crime, ceteris paribus, while increases in the gains from crime should act to increase the magnitude of criminal activity. Such an approach applied to the study of illegal behavior is not totally new, since both Beccaria and Bentham utilize an economic calculus in their early writings. Like any other kind of behavior, criminal behavior is located within a network of social organization.

Crime is always that behavior that seems to be problematic within the framework of social arrangements. For crime to be abolished, then, social arrangements themselves must also be subject to some fundamental social changes. But the core of the unwillingness to confront crime in a rational manner may be a result of our being forced to make a variety of legisltive and other decisions which we may not be prepared to make. Since a common structural feature associated with crime is the attitude and prejudice as to what crime is and does and what the criminal justice system can or should do about it, it becomes important to measure the degree to which specified changes in the operations of the criminal justice system agencies are accompanied by changes in the level of deviant behavior in the community. If we are ever to measure those communal feelings and standards, and since criminal justice is an area of strong emotions and very well entrenched in beliefs, any innovation or change must proceed slowly.

Projecting what the future moral standards will be is very difficult. We cannot quantify moral positions by the use of statistical methodologies, nor will our past history lend much in the way of allowing for any type of projection of what changes in our moral standards we can anticipate. The fluctuations in morality will impact the social structure sufficiently to show marked changes in our attitudes toward criminal behavior.

In our current symposium we do not have a presentation dealing with projections in respect either to moral value systems or political trends. Thus, there are many ways that the crime problem can be viewed. One would be the amount of damage it causes to public confidence in and respect for law and order. Another would be that the crime problem is related to the number of opportunities to commit crime. A third would be the amount of crime committed in proportion to those opportunities presented.

This whole concept of victims and victimology is one of increasing importance and I suggest that it will direct much of the thinking in the future as to the determination of crime causality. To include within these concepts of crime the notion of the victim leads to many questions about how and under what circumstances the victim may be a party to the crime; indeed under what circumstances may the victim be the cause of crime. Similarly the notion that crimes include interaction between the criminal, the victim, and the law leads immediately to questions about the role of law and and the genesis of crime, not just in defining it, but in causing it. In a like manner, once societies' agents of control are included in the definition of crime, the role of crime becomes more relevant.

CONCLUSION

One of the barriers that prevents effective criminal justice planning is the separation of powers. Legislators often appropriate funds, and then enact criminal justice statutes without considering the effects on the administration of justice. The courts, whose primary purpose is justice, are also seeing the stride of the flow of offenders. Their traditional independence has caused them to be very cautious in engaging in planning activities within the executive branch. In several cases this has led to friction within criminal justice planning bodies. Another problem in a system that is as interdependent and yet as fragmented as that of criminal justice, is the lack of overall financial coordination which leaves room for serious imbalances. The visible results are rising crime rates, court calendars, overcrowded jails, and underdeveloped diversion and prevention programs. Such conditions suggest the need for close links between criminal justice planners and those engaged in fund allocation decisions, i.e., state and local budget staffs and ultimately governors and state legislatures.

If the pervasive fragmentation of the criminal justice system into the police, courts, and correctional agencies is to be eliminated, these parts must be recognized as components of a whole. To achieve this, those concerned with criminal justice must look to systems management, systems analysis, and systems creation for aiding and integrating the parts which make up the direct delivery apparatus into one criminal justice system.

We have to look upon crime and delinquency as more than just a given to be studied and dealt with. On the contrary, it is a legislative and social construct, the nature and scope of which are subject to our determinations. Once again, the primary target for crime and delinquency policy should neither be the individual nor just the community setting, but rather the entire spectrum of the crime and delinquency defining processes themselves. "It will be through improved understanding of man and society, rather than the application of the laws of physics and chemistry, that the greatest gains will be made" (Gerald Caplan, Director, National Institute on Law Enforcement and Criminal Justice).

As planners and futurists, we must look beyond tradition and try to view the crime problem in many different ways.

A few of them that need further study are (1) measuring the amount of damage done to the public confidence in and respect for the established law and order; (2) determining the amount of loss to the victim—this is not just in terms of money, but must include resultant impact upon the psychological fear of crime; (3) looking at the crime problems as they are related to the number of opportunities available to commit crimes; and (4) a related view would be the measuring of crime committed in proportion to the opportunity.

As previously touched upon, long-range planning must take place if we are to make the proper preparations for future action. This planning must take place within a social context if it is to be realistic and effective, and there must be participation from the general citizenry. Planning cannot be left up to a few trained people; it cannot be done in a vacuum, and it must be responsive to the public.

This public responsiveness is discussed by the futurist, Alvin Toffler (1976), when he describes his concept of "Anticipatory Democracy." He talks about the workings of A/D: "So Anticipatory Democracy aims at fulfilling two needs: one, a need to involve not just so-called experts or power brokers, but rather the millions of people whose lives are effected by the consequence. When I talk about A/D, I'm talking about something for everybody—citizens futurism."

Forecasting the future is no guarantee that we will be able to meet the problems we see; but, at least, it can accomplish one thing—avoiding the fear of the unknown and unexpected.

REFERENCES

DROR, Y. (1968). "The planning process: A facet design." In Planning, programming, budgeting: A systems approach to management. Chicago: Markham.

DURKHEIM, E. (1950). Rules of sociological methods (Salvay and John Mueller, trans., G. Catlin, ed.). New York: Free Press.

——— (1964). The rules of sociological method. New York: Free Press.

JEFFERY, C.R. (1956). "The structure of American criminological thinking." Journal of Criminal Law, Criminology and Police Science, 46 (January/February):672.

KLEIN, M., KOBRIN, S., McEACHERN, A.W., SIGURDSON, H.R. (1971) "System rates: An approach to comprehensive criminal justice planning." Crime & Delinquency, 4:355-372.

SKINNER, B.F. (1971). "Beyond freedom and dignity." Psychology Today, 3(August) 37-80.

STRUENING, E.L. (1975). "Social area analysis as a method of evaluation." In E.L. Struening and M. Guttentag (eds.), Handbook of evaluation research, vol. 1. Beverly Hills, Calif.: Sage.

THOMPSON, T.M. (1972). "The criminal justice system: A view from the outside." Crime & Delinquency, (January):23-29.

TOFFLER, A. (1976). Psychology Today, (July).

VOLD, G.C. (1958). Theoretical criminology. New York: Oxford University Press.

Ronald Schneider
Florida International University
Richard Foster
Idaho State University

2

PLANNING AND DECENTRALIZATION: Can the Criminal Justice System Accommodate Both Demands?

Since the publication of the President's Crime Commission's very critical report concerning the status of the criminal justice system in America (President's Commission, 1967), articles have been appearing with increasing frequency describing this rather dismal state of affairs. Government supported research in this area has been finding, with depressing regularity, that there is, in reality, no system of criminal justice, but rather "a fragmented and often hostile amalgamation of criminal justice agencies" (National Commission, 1969:153).

One reason for this concerns the extreme geographic fragmentation of law enforcement responsibilities reflecting America's traditional desire for local autonomy. While the U.S. Constitution gives state governments the right to control law enforcement activities, "the states . . . have traditionally delegated almost all criminal justice systems' responsibilities to their subordinate local governments" (Lumbard, 1968: 890). Thus, America's system of criminal justice is

> a collectivity of some forty thousand law enforcement agencies and a multiplicity of courts, prosecution, and defense agencies, probation and parole departments, correctional institutions and related community-based organizations [Carter et al., n.d.: 1].

While this decentralization may seem to indicate many discrete systems, such is not the case. Different levels of government within the states share responsibility for different components of the system.

> States and counties remain dominant in operation of correctional institutions, counties and municipalities have prime responsibility for police activities, and states and counties shoulder the major load in operation of courts and prosecution systems [Skoler, 1968:201].

Another reason for the lack of a well-defined criminal justice system concerns the functional fragmentation of the system's components. Law enforcement, the judicial process, and corrections in the cities and states are usually autonomous bureaucracies operating at best independently and at worst actively against each other. As Daniel Freed has noted, each component of the system has different goals and sees crime from a different perspective.

> Police view their goal as apprehending criminals. They see crime in the raw and are often appalled to see courts promptly release defendants on bail, or prosecutors reduce charges, . . . or judges exclude incriminating evidence, . . . or parole officers accept supervision of released prisoners but check on them only a few minutes each month. . . . Trial judges tend to see crime for a more remote and neutral position. They see facts in dispute and two sides to each issue. . . . Judges often find law enforcement officers themselves violating the law . . . and see correctional programs as largely a failure. Corrections officials enter the crime picture long after the offense and deal only with the defendants. . . . They are discouraged when they encounter convicted persons whose sentences are either inadequate or excessive . . . They are dismayed at police officers who harass parolees, or at a community which fails to provide jobs or build halfway houses for offenders. [Freed, 1970: 266, 267]

Thus, it is not surprising to find little coordination among these various agencies. However, since they are interrelated, a change in one component of the system affects all the others. But due to the lack of communication among these agencies, changes in one subsystem are usually discovered by the remaining agencies only after the fact. Possible effects on the total system due to a change in one of its parts are rarely taken into consideration in the formulation of policy. This leads to the system's components continually reacting to each other rather than acting in concert with each other.

In response to the President's Commission's report, much of the criminological literature in recent years has stressed the necessity for comprehensive planning within the criminal justice network (Skoler, 1968; Freed, 1970; Howlett and Hurst, 1971; Hamm, 1970; Foster and Schneider, 1976; Rhodes, 1974). This notion of planning embodies two complementary concepts. Rather than viewing police, courts, and corrections as autonomous units, planning first of all requires that these agencies be viewed as components of a larger entity, the system of criminal jutice. As Carl Hamm (1970: 396) has stated, "each part of the criminal justice system must be reexamined . . . in relation to the needs of the total system." Second, the planning imperative calls for the justice network to anticipate its needs five, 10, or 20 years in the future rather than simply reacting to unforeseen circumstances as they arise. Plans must be formulated for a variety of alternative futures.

The general concept behind comprehensive planning is a relatively simple one. It first calls for careful identification of organizational goals and then requires the implementation of the most efficient means of reaching those goals. Finally, it demands constant program evaluation to determine the extent to which the objectives are being achieved.

While this may seem to be a common sense approach to decision-making, the current public desire for less centralization would appear to present a major obstacle in the path of planning's successful implementation within the criminal justice network. As even its more moderate adherents concede, comprehensive planning leads inevitably to increased centralization (Schultze, 1968:16). The need to decide on goals implies system-wide or at least agency-wide goals. And the requirement of implementing the most efficient programs to meet these goals will often require increased centralization. Clearly, for example, centralization of function may result in increased economics of scale that reduce the overall operating costs of various programs. As an example, Caputo (1976:14, 15) argues that

> if the same quality of police protection can be provided for 50,000 people at a rate of $6.75 per capita whereas it costs two jurisdictions of 25,000 each $7.75 per capita for the same services, an economy of scale exists.

Clearly, then, the cost of urban services that require expensive training and equipment may be reduced as a result of interlocal centralization because of elimination of duplication, increased purchasing power and operating efficiency, and because of the likelihood of more effective planning.

Similarly, the individual or group making decisions such as this must enjoy a position free from the parochial biases produced by occupying a post where the decisions made intimately affect the status and power of the decision maker. The logic of planning demands that system-wide decisions be made by those having system-wide responsbilities. Thus, planning implies centralization. Popular sympathies, however, appear to lie in the opposite direction. Whether these two apparently contradictory concepts can co-exist is of crucial concern if comprehensive planning is to be instituted successfully in the justice network.

At first glance the seeming agreement between citizens and administrators concerning the need for decentralization would appear to indicate a coalition of sufficient power to arrest any movement toward the centralization necessary for the successful implementation of comprehensive planning. However, this coalition is largely illusory. The reason for this apparent convergence of interests concerns the variety of meanings attributed to the concept of decentralization. As Henry Schamndt (1974) has correctly noted:

> Decentralization in its contemporary usage is a term of variable content. . . . Because everyone presumably knows what it is, little attention has been given to defining it.

At its most basic level decentralization connotes two related but conceptually distinct ideas. To most citizens it means the transfer of authority to smaller geopolitical units, i.e., community control. To administrators, however, it implies the allocation of authority and responsbility to lower echelons of the bureaucracy (Schmandt, 1974). That is, communities want control over their schools, police, and welfare agencies while administrators want to limit the restrictions imposed on them from the outside. While both citizens and bureaucrats use the same label, decentralization means very different things to each group. Lower level administrators want the freedom to formulate their own programs while the community seeks a voice in that policy formulation. Thus, although appearing harmonious, the aspirations of the two groups are fundamentally antagonistic.

Although, at first glance, the introduction of comprehensive planning would appear to satisfy neither citizens nor bureaucrats, a deeper analysis indicates that its proper application could contribute greatly to mollifying the demands of both groups. Among the private sector, the call for decentralization has come principally from those who see such a move as a means rather than an end. Those advocating greater autonomy at the local level basically want better police protection, a reduction of racial tensions, more effective education for their children, and so on. Community control is viewed primarily as a method of achieving these goals. If, however, these objectives could be reached by other means, the cries for community control should decrease substantially (Goodwin, 1969). Since comprehensive planning promises to alleviate many of the above-mentioned problems, its very implementation should reduce the desire for this type of decentralization.

As stated previously, successful implementation will require some centralization. Police, courts, and corrections must begin to work together if the problem of crime is to be reduced to manageable proportions. And it is becoming increasingly obvious that action at the state level is required. As the National Commission on the Causes and Prevention of Violence (1969) has stated:

> An assumption that parallel and overlapping public agencies will cooperate efficiently will no longer suffice as a substitute for deliberate action to make it happen.

President Johnson's unsuccessful attempts to consolidate the plethora of federal and state agencies during his drive to implement comprehensive planning at the national level might appear to indicate that similar consolidation efforts within the states might also prove futile. However, there are important legal differences between the powers of the federal government and those of the states. States are sovereign entities. They were not created and cannot be dissolved by the national government. And while the federal government has been gaining power over the states in a variety of areas, states still possess enormous spheres of autonomy which cannot be impinged upon by Washington. While Washington can offer incentives to the states to initiate one program or another, it cannot compel them to do so.

The states' legal relationship with their cities and counties is completely different. Local units are creations of the state and can, in theory, be dissolved at any time. This means that, for example, California could assume the responsibility for all law enforcement within its borders by a simple legislative act.

Consolidation attempts, however, have typically encountered political problems relating to the determination of the distribution of powers between the upper and lower tiers of government. Leaders of many interest groups or minorities, although they may recognize the fiscal and economic benefits to be gained from centralization, often oppose such proposals because they may have the effect of diluting a group's political strength by decreasing the relative proportion of the group's population vis-a-vis the entire population. In a study of attempts to develop federated metropolitan governments in the Canadian province of Ontario, a clear conclusion was that regional government implied changes that were likely to reorder many of the status and influence relationships on both the community and the individual levels.

It is this fact and the uncertainty it implies that may serve to create hostile reactions on the part of local groups, minorities, and local officials (Foster, 1974: 116-182). In addition, Luther Gulick (1962:36) provides another clear reason for the reluctance likely to be expressed by local officials over local government consolidation and reform plans.

> Each defined human institution, especially where created by law and endowed with even the smallest modicum of power, tends to develop into an independent institutional personality. This involves not only asserting itself, but also extending itself and attempting to perpetuate itself. This apparently is a law of group structure, as it is of individual existence. And among governmental institutions, the suicide complex is notably absent. . . . The existence of a fixed and immortal boundary tends to create and sustain a fixed and immortal governmental institution.

This caveat is not meant to imply that any centralization is impossible. It is only to indicate the problems that consolidation efforts may encounter. However, the total legal control over local units suggests that states are in a relatively strong position to assume the leadership in rationalizing the criminal justice process. In fact, movement in this area is beginning to occur. Eliot Lumbard (1968:890) has reported that

> a strong trend coinciding with urbanization has seen the states gradually take back many of the powers they earlier had delegated to local governments. . . . Starting first with corrections, . . . a steady and increasing state responsibility has been assumed for criminal justice system functions. That part of the system concerned with convicted offenders is primarily under state control today. Now, with mounting tempo, the trend toward state centralization of crime control functions is embracing district attorneys, the criminal courts, and increasingly, local police (commencing with training and personnel standards).

Once this functional centralization has been accomplished, nothing generic to the planning concept prevents geographical decentralization. That is, comprehensive planning does not assume that one type of strategy will achieve optimum results everywhere. In fact, it assumes nothing in this area. The call for intensive investigation of various programs for different people in a variety of locations, a basic planning tenet, might well lead to one type of correctional program for Beverly Hills, another for Boston, and still another for Harlem.

This type of flexibility, which the intelligent application of systematic analysis and comprehensive planning should produce, will also reduce the dissatisfaction of lower level administrators by increasing their freedom of action. Lower level administrators traditionally have been held accountable in terms of inputs rather than outputs. That is, instead of their evaluations being based on how much an individual contributes to the goals of the organization, his performance is measured in terms of how well he conforms to the rules designed to regulate his behavior. Given the present system, this is somewhat understandable. Upper level management quite rightly feels some responsibility to oversee the performance of their subordinates. However, due to the absence of goals and the lack of procedures designed to measure goal directed performance, some other method of control must be used. This other method invariably turns out to be "detailed regulations which rigidly specify what is 'acceptable' behavior by subordinate decisionmakers" (Schultze, 1970:152).

The intelligent use of comprehensive planning should free the lower level adminsitrator from many of the constraints placed on his behavior. Once goals are formulated, performance can be measured in terms of output. When upper level management knows what their subordinates are supposed to be achieving, they can be evaluated as to how well they are accomplishing those specified objectives. This accountability in terms of outputs rather than inputs will free the lower level manager

> from the straitjacket of input controls and promote vigorous and imaginative attempts to improve results since results will become the criteria by which they are judged. [Rivlin, 1971: 127].

Thus, the intelligent application of systematic analyis and comprehensive planning would seem to contain the capacity to alleviate many of the problems causing the demand for decentralization of the criminal justice network. Goal formulation would allow (and more likely require) a variety of programs for diverse geographic areas while, at the same time, give lower level management more freedom in designing those programs.

REFERENCES

CAPUTO, D. (1976). Urban America: The policy alternatives. San Francisco: W.H. Freeman.

CARTER, R., McEACHERN, A.W., and SIGURDSON, H. (n.d.), "Planning for criminal and juvenile justice." School of Public Administration, University of Southern California. Unpublished manuscript.

FOSTER, R.H. (1974). "Canadian intergovernmental relations and the reform of local government: Regional local government in Ontario." Unpublished Ph.D. dissertation, University of Oklahoma.

——— and SCHNEIDER, R. (1976). "Planning and the administration of justice." L.A.E. Journal, 38(January):16-22.

FREED, D. (1970). "The nonsystem of criminal justice." Pp. 263-284 in Task force on law and law enforcement, law and order reconsidered. New York: Bantam Books.

GOODWIN, R. (1969). "Sources of the public unhappiness." The New Yorker, 44 (January):38-58.

GULICK, L. (1962). The metropolitan problem and American ideas. New York: Alfred A. Knopf.

HAMM, C. (1970). "Pluralistic planning within the criminal justice system." Crime and Delinquency, 16(October):393-402.

HOWLETT, F. and HURST, H. (1971). "A systems approach to comprehensive criminal justice planning." Crime and Delinquency 17(October):345-354.

LUMBARD, E. (1969). "State and local crime control." Notre Dame Lawyer, 43(September):889-907.

National Commission on the Causes and Prevention of Violence (1969). To establish justice, to insure domestic tranquility. Washington, D.C.: U.S. Government Printing Office.

President's Commission on Law Enforcement and the Administration of Justice (1967). The challenge of crime in a free society. Washington, D.C.: U.S. Government Printing Office.

RHODES, R. (1974). "Political theory, policy analysis, and the insoluable problems of criminal justice." Policy Studies Journal, 3(Autumn):83-89.

RIVLIN, A. (1971). Systematic thinking for social action. Washington, D.C.: Brookings Institution.

SCHMANDT, H. (1974). "Decentralization: A structural imperative." In G.H. Frederickson (ed.), Neighborhood control in the 1970's: Politics, administration, and citizen participation. New York: Chandler.

SCHULTZE, C. (1968). The politics and economics of public spending. Washington, D.C.: The Brookings Institution.

——— (1970). "The role of incentives, penalties, and rewards in attaining effective policy." Pp. 145-172 in R. Haveman and J. Margolis (eds.), Public expenditures and policy analysis. Chicago: Markham.

SKOLER, D. (1968). "Comprehensive criminal justice planning: A new challenge." Crime and Delinquency, 14(July)197-206.

MARLYNN L. MAY
Beloit College

3

EDUCATION FOR CAREERS IN CRIMINAL JUSTICE: A Challenge to Liberal Arts

Since about 1970, most private liberal arts colleges have shown acute symptoms of paranoia, nostalgia, and anxiety. The *paranoia* is predicated on the perception that liberal arts is something of an anachronism in a world of specialization and narrow expertise; the *nostalgia* follows from an attempt to soothe the paranoia by harking back to the "good old days" when the liberal arts were loved and sought after; the *anxiety* sets in when nostalgia produces only momentary escapism, and the return of reality warns that there may be some basis to the parnoia. A haunting hyperconsciousness currently afoot about the vocational value of higher education—"What kind of a job will my education assure me?"—gives pause to liberal arts advocates.

With its share of these neuroses, Beloit College, a liberal arts college of approximately 1,400 full-time students, undertook a study of the relation between liberal arts education and the world of work to explore the question, "Are there problems in the structure, process, and/or substance that, if identified and changed, would make liberal arts graduates more competitive in the job market?" This essay reports on one facet of that larger study, exploring the relation between liberal arts, sociology, and criminal justice careers.

AUTHOR'S NOTE: The larger study in which this paper is based was funded by the National Science Foundation, Project Number EEP 74-18721.

Since the mid-1960s, the field of criminal justice has become increasingly professionalized. While a decade ago a high school diploma was adequate for many jobs in law enforcement and corrections (excluding the court system), this is gradually becoming less true. With the enactment of the Omnibus Crime Control and Safe Streets Act in 1968, new and large amounts of money were funneled into the Law Enforcement Education Program (LEEP), under LEAA, with the explicit purpose of encouraging personnel from all components of the criminal justice system to continue their education.

Serrill (1976:7) notes that "Since 1969, a total of $234.7 million in LEAA funds has been awarded to more than 1000 colleges and universities, many of them two-year community colleges and universities. An estimated 290,000 have gone back to school through the program . . . Most are seeking either associate or bachelor's degrees . . . This year there are a total of 100,000 people in the program, including 12,000 corrections personnel." In addition, increasing numbers of those who are college undergraduates have become "converts" to criminal justice as a possible future career.

To meet these increasing demands many colleges and universities have created new criminal justice programs, concentrated largely at the undergraduate level.[1] At the same time, requirements for jobs were being upgraded and specialized across the nation, though not by any means at the same rate as the educational development. At present, then, it is possible to enter the criminal justice field with (1) a high school diploma; (2) an Associate of Arts degree; (3) a Bachelor of Science degree in Criminal Justice (four-year specialized); (4) a Bachelor of Arts degree, usually with a social science major; (5) a Master's degree in Criminal Justice (or related social service field); and (6) a Ph.D. degree in Criminal Justice. It is apparant that four of the six are specialized degrees *aimed specifically* at careers in the criminal justice field. On the surface, the liberal arts graduate is in a less than favorable position.

But other considerations from another perspective make the liberal arts graduate's position less bleak. First, liberal arts graduates have two options: either seek a job in the criminal justice field directly out of college, or opt for getting an advanced degree in criminal justice. Invariably, in interviews with faculty and adminstrators of graduate programs, it became clear that they want academically well-rounded and qualified students; to wit, "the students who come from a liberal arts background are (1) better students, (2) can write better, and (3) are better analytically and qualitatively." Opting for the advanced degree puts the liberal arts graduate with a respectable GPA from an excellent liberal arts college in a choice, competitive position for the M.A. and Ph.D. degree programs. Furthermore, to pursue a graduate degree is generally advantageous, because as the criminal justice field becomes glutted with job candidates academic degrees will inflate, making the M.A. degree more marketable. Moreover, as the field continues to professionalize, job specifications will include advanced degree work as a basic requirement, most likely even for the lower level entrants. Consider, for example, that in the Federal Bureau of Prisons during the 1974-1975 fiscal year, 75% of those applying for correctional officer jobs (guards) in the system had bachelor's degrees.

Nevertheless, the advanced degree option at present is *not* the only one available for career entry from liberal arts. The option of seeking a job in criminal justice directly out of college is still modestly salient. However, if this choice is made, liberal arts graduates will be competing most directly with the B.S. degree graduates in criminal justice. The reasons for this are as follows: (1) the liberal arts graduate is obviously not qualitatively competitive with the Ph.D., since the Ph.D. qualifies the holder for jobs not within the specifications of a B.A. degree holder; (2) the M.A. will almost always take precedence over either a B.S. or B.A. degree, though competing for the same jobs; (3) the liberal arts graduate will take precedence over the A.A. degree holder, since the A.A. degree will increasingly become substantively too confining; and finally (4) the high school diploma is slowly but deliberately being shunted out of the market.[2]

By a simple process of credential elimination, therefore, the liberal arts graduate not wishing to seek a graduate degree will have stiffest competition with the B.S. degree graduates. Yet it is by no means a foregone conclusion that the liberal arts graduate will lose out. The success or failure in procuring a job will hinge, in large part, on two important factors: (1) the professional perspectives of the hiring agency and staff, in correlation with (2) the qualitative nature of the two degrees.

Among the top decision makers, planners, administrators, and academicians the professionalization of criminal justice is seen as a must, *but* it is *not always the case* that agency staff are as aware or concerned with it. On the one hand, some agency staff are not fully aware of *what* a B.S. or M.A. in criminal justice signifies. On the other hand, some who are aware of the professional upgrading are not in agreement with the movement and may resist it for a time.[3] The liberal arts graduate who understands this, and takes seriously the findings presented in this paper, has important clout for entering a criminal justice career directly from college.

But even in situations where agency staff are aware of the B.S. degree and consider it in hiring, two factors have troubled its consideration. First, because the LEEP monies came so quickly, with an urgency to "get on the road," many of the B.S. programs were constructed rapidly, and haphazardly. This resulted in courses, faculty, and curricula "created" without time taken to think them through, or to consider their place in the larger academic context. Few academicians specifically trained to teach criminal justice were available. Either faculty trained in other disciplines and specialties were "borrowed" and asked to apply their training to criminal justice, or practitioners were brought in from the field on a part-time basis. They know their specific jobs technically, but often had a less than comprehensive understanding of the total criminal justice system and lacked a theoretical and philosophical knowledge of criminal justice.[4]

A second difficulty concerns the narrowness of the focus in the B.S. degree. Too few B.S. degree programs have required broadly based course distribution requirements, instead focusing the student in courses dealing too completely with technical proficiency. The result: highly specialized and narrowly focused graduates at a very early stage of their own life development. Because the criminal justice field is changing rapidly, narrowly focused training tends to diminish the graduates' ability to be flexible and deal with change effectively. Furthermore, the graduates, not having a broadly based education, lack a comprehensive perspective on themselves in the larger society. Both of these factors set up potential for "dead ending" and "burn out." Finally, the B.S. degree graduate with a relatively narrow technical training tends to lack a comprehensive understanding of the criminal justice *system*, creating expectations for too much advancement, too fast, and with too few results, exacerbating the burn out potential.

Within this context, what are the advantages and disadvantages of the liberal arts graduate? The major disadvantage comes from not having as much specific, technical knowledge about criminal justice as the B.S. graduate. A major advantage, however, is inherent in the nature of the liberal arts education. For years, the proponents of liberal arts have argued for, and prided themselves in, preparing students broadly and deeply to understand themselves in a comprehensive way as self-actualizing, independent participants in a maze of social institutions. This approach to education provides a perspective on self, institutional stuctures and processes, and profession, enabling the individual *not only to survive, but to thrive* in a system of bureaucratic structures and processes that have fragmentized, specialized, and compartmentalized the individual into discretely functioning parts.

The timelessness of this perspective on education is emphasized in the interviews. Time and again questions are raised about what exactly professional criminal justice education should prepare professionals to be. On the one hand, should professional education be focused essentially on preparing students to "fill the slots" that may or may not be available upon graduation? Or, is the purpose of education to prepare individuals who will be leaders, have a comprehensive understanding of criminal justice, and have at least the rudimentary special skills and general knowledge to create viable change? A critical concern about the nature, direction, and means of change weaves through the interviews. Lack of knowledge about political, economic, and social processes and structures concerns educators and employers, often articulated as a concern for a lack of understanding about *how* to bring about change, and about *why* changes are important. Too narrow, specialized educational and professional focus results in either criminal justice professionals who are "joiners," becoming primarily bureaucratic functionaries, or who are "naive innovators," lacking a knowledge of organizational structure, process, and change to substantiate their innovative desires.

A second major advantage for liberal arts graduates appears. In interviews, particularly with agency staff, three basic skills are identified and considered essential in people they hire: (1) ability to write well; (2) ability to verbalize well; and (3) ability for logical, analytical, and critical thought. Writing skills are essential because so much of the work in the system requires written communications. The "memo" is a way of life, and it must be done with clarity, conciseness, and logic, in such a way as to persuade as well as well inform. Once the message has been written and the supervisor follows up, it becomes crucial for the professional to be skilled in orally explaining and arguing a point critically, logically, and with believability. While any system will have its places for those who can simply follow orders, the person who is heard and seen is the one who can (a) think through problems clearly and suggest alternatives (the problem solver), and (b) take another's ideas and critically analyze them, pointing out weaknesses and strengths. All of these skills are basic if the individual is to thrive creatively on the system rather than simply survive in it. Here the liberal arts graduate should be a genuine competitor. Writing, oral articulation, and critical analysis are major tools in the liberal arts curriculum, and the ones so often mentioned as lacking in the survival kits of the B.S. graduate in criminal justice.

Invariably in the interviews the topic of "who gets the jobs?" arises and leads to the counsel that knowing what your assets are for the job wanted is paramount. The persons who are most aggressive in articulating specifically what they want in a job, know exactly what their educational and personal assets are, and know how to "sell" those assets to the employer are the ones who get the job—what some call "showing initiative."

This is wisdom particularly pertinent to liberal arts. Yet here is where the liberal arts faculty and students have too often fallen short, allowing themselves to be neutralized by a society preaching technique and specialization. The very educational process in liberal arts emphasizes initiative—initiative directed toward the development of intellectual and critical capacities, but certainly toward one's own personal development as well. This should be articulated and conveyed wisely and persuasively.

Finally, experience is constantly emphasized as an important factor essential in seeking and procuring the first job. It seems that *any* amount of experience would be of value, but the more the better. The experience may be directly in criminal justice, or in some related social service fields. This fact has significant implications for the curriculum and teaching methods in liberal arts and will be discussed below.

II

What are some implications of these findings for liberal arts?

Precipitant Majors

If the liberal arts graduate cannot garner the same degree of technical knowledge as the B.S. degree competitor, there *are* some types of curricular preparations that will help the liberal arts graduate be more competitive. As one might expect, a social science background is important. But even more pointedly, a major in Sociology and/or Political Science stands out as most competitive.

Why Sociology and/or Political Science? First, criminal justice is being understood more than ever before as *a systemic process and function,* with diminished importance placed on the independent functioning of each of the components in the system. Each institutional component, its organizational structure, and the professionals within are understood to share goals and methods that integratedly work to affect criminal justice in the whole. Second, with the systemic perspective comes increased emphasis on the political elements in criminal justice. Our crime control system is a "legal" one in the sense that it is bounded by statutory law, by appellate court decisions, and structurally rests on sources of authority from all branches of government—legislative, judical, and executive. Third, there is accordingly a movement away from such a strong emphasis on "individual treatment" modalities. Individual treatment is not disappearing entirely, but is being modulated by the perspectives of complex organization—political, social, and economic.

With these three "shifts" the significance of a Sociology and/or Political Science major becomes apparent. Focusing on the inextricable bond of the individual social, political, and economic institutions in society, special emphasis is given by these disciplines to the ways in which institutions and the individual are in a constant dialectical tension. Included in this understanding is a significant appreciation of the effects of social systems on the individual that is not as clearly present in psychology or other social sciences.

Curriculum

Sociology[5] in the liberal arts college should continue to provide as rich a fare of offering as possible and not attempt to develop a professionally specialized program designed for criminal justice training. The reasons for this are inherent in the discussion above and in the fact that the nature of liberal arts education is opposed to premature narrowing and specialization.

But the Sociology curriculum *can* do four things for the liberal arts graduate. First, it should include substantial courses, taught rigorously, in theory and concepts related to the criminal justice field, e.g., criminology, sociology of law, deviance and control, and juvenile delinquency. These courses can then be put into a *critical* context by other courses providing more general bases for analyses of society and the individual, e.g., political sociology, stratification, social systems, urban communities, self and social structure, and collective behavior. Where possible, these two sets of courses ought to be interwoven, integrating the more general sociological theory and concepts with the more specific content of courses related to criminal justice. For example, a "senior seminar" designed with faculty, students, and professionals from the field sharing theoretical, research, work, and ethical concerns would enhance the students' understanding of and progress toward a career in criminal justice.

Second, a serious attempt to relate classroom work to some measure of "on-line" work experience as an integral part of the learning process is needed. This in no way means that courses should become primarily "practicum" courses. High standards must be maintained theoretically, analytically, and critically, a forte of the liberal arts education not to be forfeited to exclusive experiential education. But the experience should be in a professional agency for a full academic term at a time. Field trips, or a few days of observation, do not fulfill the definition of "experience." The student should be a *significant* actor in the on-line experience, participating with a practitioner, preferably being supervised and evaluated by both practitioner and faculty. And the faculty member's involvement is significant. Generating significant on-line opportunities demands long, hard hours of faculty time with a sensitivity to the world outside academe. The benefits are substantial because they hold the potential for faculty conversion." For the first time, some faculty will discover the finely integrated relation between knowledge and action. Students gain the important competitive ingredient of significant "experience" to be used in seeking the first job and will also have acquired important contacts in the work world for those all-important references.

A problem: some liberal arts colleges are not situated in urban centers or semiurban communities providing outlets needed for such involvement. The alternative is to seek complementary forms, for example some form of urban studies program, preferably taking the student off campus and into a major metropolitan center. One exemplary program is operated by the Associated Colleges of the Midwest (ACM), based in Chicago, and not connected with a university. This program offers students opportunities to study and work in a potential career option, with the staff acting as catalysts enabling students to be reflectively critical about what they are experiencing and learning vis-à-vis self, education, and career. Many a career option has been made or dropped because of this experience, and certainly the work experience while on the program is highly favorable on the graduate's job application and vita.

Third, the Sociology curriculum must contain *at least one* rigorous course in research methods and design. Methods and design act as a mini-logic course, forcing the student to think clearly and logically and to develop problem-solving skills; and increasingly, research skills are required in the field of criminal justice. A student who has skills in methodology will be in a favored position. In addition, at least one statistics course to back up the methodology plus a course in computer design and analysis would be excellent.

Fourth, the Sociology curriculum must find a way to make sociological theory work for the students, in two ways. First, well-taught courses cannot simply "teach sociological theory" as an objective form of knowledge, but must demand that the students put the theory to work on their own life contexts, on their own career futures. By so doing, students can appraise the potentialities and pitfalls that they will have to face in the job system. Second, and closely related, theory and concepts "put to work" will give the student a concrete *and* theoretical understanding not only of how social structures and systems work, but how they can be *made to work for* the individual as well as against the individual. Theories and concepts placed in a concrete, working context, enhance students' staying power for thriving in the system, criticizing and recreating it, and making it possible for them to play the roles rather than have the roles play them.

Teaching Method

Given the fact that three skills—writing, verbal, and critical/analytical skills—are highly prized in criminal justice, two pedagogical methods become crucial in teaching and learning. First, classroom learning and teaching should be built around a discussion/seminar format, with its primary forte being the demand that students not only think critically, concisely, and logically, but that they articulate their ideas just as critically, concisely, and logically, "I can think it, but I just can't say it" will not suffice. This pedagogy also will enable students to build confidence in themselves and to value their ideas, a major plus in competing for jobs and then thirving on the job. Further, critical paper writing and essay exams are paramount. As traditional as these forms are, they continue to be extremely important vehicles for preparing students for the work world. Faculty who evaluate papers and exams only on the basis of content and not for writing ability as well are doing their students a disservice.

Advising

Finally, student advising has become highly significant. Advising has to begin at early stages in the college career and be done on three levels.

At the first level, advising should articulate a clear understanding of the significance of a liberal arts education and the advantages it has *for* the work world. The present failure to do this is one of the most dismal failures of which liberal arts faculty and administration are guilty. In part, the failure is due to too hearty a belief that the past will carry the present (the nostalgia fallacy). But the reality of the present situation is that while the liberal arts education is still just as viable and valuable *in itself* as it always was, the society around liberal arts has changed its apparent needs for the time being. Liberal arts is made to look and feel like a billiard ball on a pool table in a society emphasizing technical skill and specialization. Therefore, those who conscientiously believe that liberal arts has significant value must create opportunites to interpret that belief into clear and logical rationales for students and employers. "Interpreting" liberal arts enables students to develop a confidence in their education first, and then its value in the work world.

This first level of advising must be supported by a second, advising containing technical abilities in how to go about the job search. It will include training designed to help the student develop (1) a well-defined set of career goals and the kind(s) of job(s) wanted, and (2) an ability to be assertive and independent. Advising that enhance in this direction will move students out and have them talking with people outside academia, in the halls and offices of people in typical job settings. Knowledge of the work world, personal assertiveness, and independence for the students will be the result.

A third level of advising is concerned particularly with what courses to take and what work experiences to gain. In this vein, alternative course groupings (tracks) can be developed that pertain to specific careers. Such "tracks" would include not only courses in Sociology, but courses chosen from other relevant departmental offerings in the college. This does not necessitate nor recommend developing a submajor in criminal justice within Sociology. But advising on courses and course groupings does help clarify for the students the logic encircling their criminal justice interests and show them how a Sociology major, in concert with other courses from other departments, can support their career interests.

Conclusion

Time and again in the interviews, the message comes through that liberal arts has sold itself short. Identify the "assets" intrinsic to the liberal arts education, become convinced of the value of that education in itself and for the work world, and then convey it to the employer of their choice it was argued. The liberal arts graduate who does this will sustain a perspective on self and society to be continuously recreating both, will have learned the fine continuously recreating both, will have learned the fine art of being thrivers and not only survivors, and *is* employable.

NOTES

1. For specific information to appraise the issue of education in criminal justice, the following apply: (1) "*Law Enforcement and Criminal Justice Education—Directory, 1975-1976*" can be ordered from The International Association of Chiefs of Police, Professional Standards Division, Gaithersburg, Maryland; and (2) "*Criminal Justice Graduate Programs Catalogue,*" and "*Supplement No. 1*" can be ordered from the Office of the Coordinator, National Criminal Justice Educational Consortium, Academic Services Building, No. 306, Arizona State University, Tempe, Arizona 85281. For more general discussions of education and criminal justice, see the following: (1) Senna (1974:389-397), (2) Klyman and Karman (1974:398-404), (3) Newman (1974), and (4) "*Criminology and Corrections Programs: A Study of the Issues,*" can be ordered from the American Correctional Association, 4321 Hartwick Rd., Suite L-208, College Park, Maryland 20740.

2. It will gradually go by the way as "more educated" people glut the market, forcing the salary scale down enough to make the "more educated" employable at wage scales commensurate with those now paid the high school graduates, and as standards for jobs become upgraded and stabilized nationwide.

3. One indication of this is a movement among practitioners, particularly in corrections and law enforcement, to unionize to protect against loss of jobs, even when new standards are not met by present personnel.

4. For a thoughtful critique and analysis with recommendations concerning the place, function, and structure of criminal justice bachelor degree programs in the educational system, see Newman (1974). In addition, for a view on the current debate taking place over these new programs, see Serrill (1976:7,10).

5. The discussion to follow focuses primarily on implications for liberal arts sociology majors, because my investigations and attempts to apply the findings have been within this discipline.

REFERENCES

American Correctional Association (n.d). "Criminology and corrections programs: A study of the issues." College Park, Md.: Author.

International Association of Chiefs of Police (1975-1976). "Law enforcement and criminal justice education." Gaithersburg, Md.: Author.

KLYMAN, F.I. and KARMAN, T.A. (1974). "A perspective for graduate-level education in criminal justice." Crime & Delinquency, 20(October):398-404.

National Criminal Justice Educational Consortium (n.d.). "Criminal justice graduate programs catalogue." Tempe, Ariz.: Author.

NEWMAN, D. (1974). Criminal justice education in Wisconsin. Albany: State University of New York. Unpublished manuscript.

SENNA, J.J. (1974) "Criminal justice higher education—Its growth and directions." Crime & Delinquency, 20(October):389-397.

SERRILL, M.S. (1976). "LEAA: A question of impact." Corrections Magazine, 2(June):3-12, 17-29.

Robert H. Aronson
University of Washington

4

TOWARD A RATIONAL RESOLUTION OF ETHICAL DILEMMAS IN THE CRIMINAL JUSTICE SYSTEM

Former Vice President Agnew's "post-Watergate morality" has engendered an overwhelming interest within the legal profession in professional responsibility and legal ethics. The number of attorneys who knowingly committed crimes was upsetting, to be sure, but they could be handled like all others who break the law for private gain or power or prestige.

Of greater concern, however, to those in the legal profession who believe that the preeminent place of lawyers in our society mandates that their behavior be above reproach, were the lawyers who contributed to the illegality by preparing documents, refusing to reveal what they knew—even delivering packages at their client's bidding, which were found to contain "hush money."

This latter group of attorneys often believed that they were performing ethically under the Adversary System, and some legal commentators agreed. No one was certain how widely held this conception of legal ethics was, but it was clear that something had to be done.

AUTHOR'S NOTE: This paper is a modification and condensation of a more detailed analysis in the *Washington Law Review* (1976:273-320), entitled "Professional Responsibility: Education and Enforcement."

Legal ethics, not even taught in some law schools, became an important, often required, part of the law school curriculum. Bar Association grievance committees sought new, more effective ways of discovering and disciplining unethical conduct in the legal profession.

But the efforts toward education and discipline have not produced the hoped-for confidence in the ethical conduct of lawyers, and that is because there remains fundamental disagreement within the profession concerning the proper functioning of attorneys under the Adversary System.

This is particularly true of lawyers—prosecutors and defense attorneys—involved in the criminal justice system, and may be illustrated by a recent cause célèbre in New York. Appointed attorneys representing an indigent learned that their client had not only committed the murder of which he was accused but two others as well (People v. Belge, 1975). The two victims had been missing for many months, and the fact of their murders was unknown. The client gave the lawyers sufficient information to discover the bodies. At this point, a layperson would surely think that the public interest would demand disclosure of these crimes, and certainly any decent person would desire to disclose them. But the lawyers, despite such a desire, felt bound by Canon 4 of the ABA Code of Professional Responsibility which states that "A Lawyer Should Preserve the Confidences and Secrets of a Client,"[1] and did not reveal what they knew. This rule expresses the public interest in maintaining the almost sacred trust between lawyer and client which enables the work of the law to progress because clients will candidly disclose their affairs. Yet one of the footnotes to the rule of confidentiality states that "[p]ublic policy forbids that the relation of attorney and client should be used to conceal wrongdoing," and that "a communication by a client to his attorney in respect to . . . a continuing wrong is not privileged from disclosure."[2]

Unfortunately, the mode of analysis by which these lawyers were to define and weigh the public interest in their case was unclear. Technically, within the explicit dictates of the Code, there was no future or ongoing "wrongdoing" in the sense of criminal activity. But neither were the murders a *fait accompli*, since the parents and police were continuing the search for the missing persons not yet known to be dead. Much "wrongdoing" in the sense of added suffering and expense was ongoing due to the silence of the lawyers involved. It would seem that at the very least the attorneys should have informed the parents or police anonymously of the death or whereabouts of the victims through as many intermediaries as was necessary to protect their client.

And, just as the specifically applicable provision of the lawyers' Code of Legal Ethics was ambiguous, neither was there a "guiding principle" to which the attorneys could turn for the answer.

Criminal lawyers are told that they have a duty to their clients, to the legal profession, and to society as a whole.[3] **In a very few instances, these duties do conflict—e.g., a** lawyer shall not engage in "illegal conduct involving moral turpitude."[4] When they do conflict, however, a search of the relevant state code usually reveals no more guidance than to "do the right thing" under the circumstances. The attorney is not told which of the conflicting duties is deemed to be of greater importance or given an ultimate goal or legal theory to apply. These problems of determining and enforcing professional responsibility under the Code are an inevitable by-product of a situation-oriented approach to the analysis of ethical dilemmas.

No one would think of promulgating a criminal code which instructed citizens to do what was best for themselves, their friends, relatives and neighbors, and society as a whole. Even more unthinkable would be to employ a "good faith" test to determine whether this ambiguous "rule" had been violated. And yet, that is exactly what we do with respect to lawyers, particularly those operating within the criminal justice system. The model under which they must perform is what I call the "Situation Model."

The essence of this model is that each situation in which an ethical question is presented is unique. The situation may demand primacy for the truth, or for maintenance of the Adversary System, or for the attorney's personal ethics, or for other goals relevant only to the particular problem. A uniform goal orientation is subordinated to reaching the "right" result in each case.

Thus, had the two New York lawyers looked to provisions in the ABA Code concerning the relative values of duty to client and duty to society, they would have found that the goal of preserving the lawyer-client privilege, with its concomitants of encouraging trust and candor, is paramount in the situation where the client admits committing the crime charged. There is an absolute duty on the attorney not to reveal in any way what has been learned, no matter what the client's admission indicates about the future dangerousness of the client (short of criminal acts), nor how personally distressing it may be to the lawyer to conceal the knowledge.[5] But this interest in protecting the relationship of the lawyer and client disappears when the client reveals an intention to commit another crime. In this situation, the Code suggests that the lawyer consider first the protection of the public and second his or her own integrity.[6] Knowledge of an intent to commit a crime thus calls for radically different behavior on the part of the lawyer, even though revelation of the client's confidence will be equally destructive of the relationship in either case. The situational model is, in effect, a balancing test, which has intuitive appeal (Carlin and Howard, 1965).

But because the individual attorney is the final arbiter of what is "right" in close cases, his or her decision is virtually unreviewable. It is like telling a poor man whose family is sick and starving that two of the primary goals of society are life and to heal the sick, and that it is particularly noble to do both at great risk to oneself; but that also to steal is evil and a threat to society; and then tell the man to decide for himself whether stealing necessary drugs from a pharmacy is "right" or "wrong" under the circumstances. And, whatever he concludes, if he acts in good faith, the law will take no punitive action!

The reason that this result seems so absurd is that the criminal law, unlike ethical codes for criminal lawyers, is founded on a System Model. Criminologists, lawyers, judges, and legislators have considered the various goals of the criminal law and have enacted laws which tell people which goals have been determined to be foremost in controlling behavior.

One such guiding principle is that stealing is wrong, no matter how compelling the motive for the theft.

It is against the law to steal because of greed, but it is also illegal for the police to steal in order to catch a murderer, or for the president to burglarize a psychiatrist's files to protect "national security." And "good faith" is not an adequate defense. It is the guiding principle which controls, not some ambiguous balancing test.

A similar mode of analysis should be applicable to criminal lawyers under a System Model of legal ethics. Such a model would define the lawyer's role in terms of the legal system's overall goals. The lawyer's primary function would be to serve those goals to the best of his or her ability regardless of personal ethics. The duty as a member of the legal profession to subordinate personal morality for the good of the system is not an adoption of the maxim "the end justifies the means." Rather, it calls for awareness of the fact that each ethical dilemma does not stand on its own as a discrete entity, unrelated to other parts of the system, and recognition that choosing the "best" or most ethical course of action in a given situation might have an adverse, "unethical" effect somewhere else in the system.

Take, for example, the case of the lawyer who, through skilled representation, obtains acquittal for a person who has committed a heinous crime. Since the Constitution entitles one accused of a crime to counsel, it is axiomatically ethical under our criminal justice system to act as his counsel, no matter how horrible his crime or how "guilty" or unpopular he may be.[7] The attorney who attempts to exonerate one he knows to be guilty is no less ethical than the prosecutor who seeks to effect his conviction. Both are equally necessary to the proper functioning of the system.

Admittedly, there are essential functions which the defense attorney does not perform. But that is why the system provides police, prosecutor, judge, and jury. Therefore, an attorney who uses his skills on behalf of a "guilty" client acts properly with respect to the system. One who does less for such a client than he would do for "innocent" or popular clients improperly permits personal ethical beliefs to take precedence over professional responsibility. The goal of the system is achieved only because the attorney performs in a manner which might otherwise be perceived as unethical if considered in isolation.

Because the system model defines professional responsibility in individual cases in terms of a goal or guiding principle, it is essential that the Bar achieve consensus as to the overall goal of each subpart of the system of justice. The two most widely accepted goals of the system, each often dictating somewhat different behaviors in different situations, are truth-oriented and adversary-oriented, with a subclass of the latter applying only to criminal justice: innocence-oriented.

It may be helpful to illustrate the operation of these models, and indicate how the New York attorneys could have resolved their dilemma under each.

First, under the truth-oriented model the Anglo-American trial is seen as a process "within which man's capacity for impartial judgment can attain its fullest realization" (ABA Journal, 1958), and the function of the advocate is "to assist the trier of fact in making this impartial judgment" (Noonan, 1966).[8] On a practical level, extensive discovery procedures for civil litigation and the easing of barriers to pretrial discovery in criminal law aid in implementing the truth-oriented model. Partisan advocacy is appropriate only insofar as it aids in the correct adjudication of the facts; when it "misleads, distorts and obfuscates," it is unacceptable (ABA Journal, 1958). As Chief Justice Warren Burger has stated: "The lawyer gives to his client the benefit of his learning, his talents, and his judgment, but he never forgets what he owes to himself and to others . . . He has a prior and perpetual retainer on behalf of truth and justice.

He is the professional representative but not the alter ego of his client.[9]

Thus, the New York attorneys' decision of whether to reveal the existence of the missing bodies, so difficult to resolve under the Situation Model, is easily resolved under the Truth Model. Since discovery of truth is the overriding goal, a lawyer would clearly have a duty to reveal the fact of the murders, whether anonymously or not.

The Adversary Model, on the other hand, leaves Truth to the trier of fact, the judge or the jury. The attorneys on each side of the dispute investigate, introduce, and argue the evidence most favorable to their own side. This method of presentation avoids the natural tendency to "judge too swiftly in terms of the familiar that which is not yet fully known" (ABA Journal, 1958:1159). No matter how great an effort one makes to remain neutral, past experience, subconscious biases, and preconceptions formed from preliminary investigations inevitably lead to prejudgment (Fuller, 1961). Once a number of facts indicate guilt, for example, the virtually irresistible tendency is to find additional evidence substantiating the initial judgment. Contrary evidence or testimony is thereafter not as actively pursued. The Adversary System recognizes this psychological tendency, but avoids its dysfunctional aspects by instructing each side of a dispute to form a bias and pursue all facts, testimony, legal precedents, and arguments in its favor, and attack all evidence and arguments for the opposing side. Through partisan advocacy, both sides are fully presented to a trier of fact (Freedman, 1967).

A second function served by the adversary process of adjudication is not only to ensure that justice in fact *has* been done, but that it also *appears* to have been done. To the extent that trials take the place of self-help by wronged individuals, to the extent that rehabilitation of criminal offenders requires that those convicted believe themselves to have been tried fairly, and to the extent that the orderly functioning of government and protection against resort to violence require faith in the integrity of the legal system, it is essential that all sides in a controversy be seen to have been adequately represented. This function is aided, particularly with respect to the accused in a criminal trial, by providing a partisan advocate on either side of the controversy.

One way of ensuring the effective and enthusiastic representation of the criminal accused is by providing him or her a representative who does not act according to a personal opinion, but rather assumes innocence and acts as an advocate to promote that view. In addition, the lawyer must not reveal his client's confidences, and must do nothing to aid the prosecution. The prosecution has a reservoir of attorneys and investigators, the accused has only one defender.

Thus, under the Adversary Model, the lawyer faced with a dilemma like that of the two New York attorneys would ask how the goals of the Adversary System would best be furthered. Since the system can operate only if the relationship of trust and candor between lawyer and client is given priority, the lawyers would be bound to withhold the information about the missing bodies.[10]

As our system is presently constituted, however, neither of these models has been chosen. Despite our interest in truth, "no lawyer would consider it unethical to prevent the introduction of evidence such as a murder weapon seized in violation of the fourth amendment or a truthful but involuntary confession, or to defend a guilty man on grounds of denial of a speedy trial. Such are permissible because there are policy considerations that at times justify frustrating the search for truth and the prosecution of a just claim" (Freedman, 1966).

Likewise, despite our interest in the adversary system and the presumption of innocence, we do very little to ensure that the combatants are of equal ability. If the prosecutor's office, with all of its resources, is able to more fully develop and present its side of the case than defense counsel, the fact finder is deprived of the necessary information to arrive at the correct decision.

In other words, the Adversary Model contemplates adversaries of equal ability and resources. In reality, however, not only the resources, but the disparate abilities of prosecution and defense attorneys indicate that the notion of achieving Justice through the Adversary Model is presently an illusion. The standard is not whether defense counsel has done an effective or even creditable job, but whether the representation has been so poor as to constitute a farce or mockery of justice so as to shock the conscience of the court.[11] Although the modern trend has been to require a higher standard of performance,[12] no court has yet required representation even roughly equal to that of the prosecution.

And, even more important, a substantial portion of the Bar still considers it ethical for defense counsel to do less for a client he believes to be guilty than he would for one he believes to be innocent. For example, in one case,[13] counsel induced the defendant to plead guilty to three murders and a number of assaults and refused to raise an insanity defense, despite a weak prosecution case and counsel's own "doubts as to this defendant's mental capacity for crime."[14] The defendant had been subjected to every kind of coercion and interrogation, including illegal search of his living quarters, four days of continuous questioning, and the use of sodium pentothal and lie detector tests, resulting in what would have been inadmissible real evidence and an inadmissible confession. Despite this treatment and psychiatric evidence suggesting mental instability, defense counsel repeatedly urged a guilty plea because he and the prosecuting attorney "were collectively agreed that any thought on the part of the State to cause this man to forfeit his life would be unjust. It would be unfair. By the same token we were collectively agreed that any course on our part which would assist in having him returned to society would be equally unfair."[15]

In acknowledging defense counsel's "cooperative assistance" to the court, the prosecutor stated that without defense counsel's aid, "to this day a great and sincere public doubt might remain as to the guilt of [the defendant]."[16]

Although the court refused to reverse the defendant's conviction on his guilty plea because the representation was not "of such low caliber as to be equivalent to no representation at all,"[17] it is clear that counsel's first loyalty was to his own conscience and moral beliefs, rather than to his client's interest in obtaining the best treatment permitted under the law. And that was just one instance where an attorney's devotion to truth and his own integrity subverted the Adversary Model of justice.[18] It is also an example of the need for the legal profession to provide better guidance with respect to the proper resolution of conflicts between loyalty to one's client and loyalty to the truth.

The definition and enforcement of lawyers' professional responsibility is in great need of revision. The failure to develop and adopt a consistent formulation of ethical duty has resulted in a set of ambiguous and contradictory rules as well as the inability to impose discipline effectively in all but instances of the most egregious misconduct. The academic debate has gone on too long.[19] Meaningful choices regarding systems of defining and regulating professional responsibility *can* be made. If the legal profession is to continue to be self-monitoring it must discard the Situation-oriented Model for one that is System-oriented.

Attorneys must decide what goals are to be given priority in these cases of conflict. If an equal adversary system is the best means of attaining justice, then *all* rules of conduct must promote that system. A true adversary system may dictate that all lawyers be assigned to indigents and unpopular cases because the interest in permitting them totally free choice is subordinate to the need for the adversaries to be equal. If we are truly to have an innocence-oriented system of criminal justice, then we must stop treating criminal defense attorneys as somewhat soiled and instead develop rules which not only permit but demand that all conduct be consistent with a belief in the innocence of an accused. An attorney who reveals confidences because of a perceived duty to the court, or negotiates a plea in the belief that a duty is owed to society to keep the client off the streets, will be deemed to have acted unethically.

If, on the other hand, we are to accept the search for truth as the overriding goal of the legal system, then the attorney-client privilege must be severely limited, the maximum pretrial discovery constitutionally permissible (both civil and criminal) must be required and enforced, the role of the trial judge must be greatly expanded, and decisions based on "loopholes and technicalities" must be greatly reduced.

It may not be possible to adopt any of the models *in toto*. It may be necessary or desirable to adopt a truth-oriented model in civil litigation and an Adversary Model in the criminal justice system. Or the attorney as counselor might be required to act under the rules designed to promote the search for truth, whereas the conduct of lawyers as advocates would be dictated by adversary principles. Decisions such as these must be made by the legal profession as a body and not according to the personal balancing test of each individual member of the Bar. Once the decision has been made, all attorneys should be bound by their associates' judgments.

For each of the models discussed, the primary goal should be that of justice. Often the models overlap, but always an attorney can resolve doubts by attempting to achieve truth or a fairly balanced adversary procedure, or treatment of an accused which comports with innocence until proven guilty.

The overall operation of the system can be handled by mechanisms to change particular dysfunctional results. Without some guiding principle or framework, however, ethical decisions will continue to be made within the framework of attorneys' individual consciences, and after-the-fact review and discipline will continue to be both arbitrary and unjust.

NOTES

1. American Bar Association Code of Professional Responsibility; see Disciplinary Rule 4-101. Cal. Bus. and Prof. Code § 6068(e) (West 1974) provides: "It is the duty of an attorney . . . to maintain inviolate the confidence, and at every peril to himself to preserve the secrets, of his client."

2. ABA Code at 18 n.15 (footnote to DR 4-101(C)(2) quoting ABA Comm. on Professional Ethics, Opinions, No. 156 [1936]).

3. "Preamble" and "Preliminary Statement" to ABA Code at page 1. See generally ABA Code Canons 4,5,6,&7 (duty to client); 1,2,8 (duty to legal profession); 3,9 (duty to public).

4. ABA Code, DR 1-102(A)(3).

5. ABA Code, DR 4-101(B). See EC 4-4, EC 4-5.

6. See ABA Code, DR 4-101(C)(3).

7. This position is reflected in the ABA Code. ABA Code, EC 2-27, EC 2-29.

8. See also Bress (1966), "All lawyers must remember that the basic purpose of the trial is the determination of truth."

9. Burger (1966), quoting an unidentified "great British barrister, later a judge." See also Drinker (1952).

10. The only accommodation the lawyer might make within this model is to seek the client's consent to an anonymous revelation not linked to the client. In other words, it might be possible to reveal the information about the fact of the murders without revealing the implication from the client's own words that he was responsible for them. Revealing the second piece of information would be unacceptable in the adversary oriented model.

11. United States v. Sanchez (1973), Hayes v. Russell (1969), Davis v. Bomar (1965). See also Bazelon (1973).

12. Herring v. Estelle (1974), see also Brown v. Swenson (1973). and United States v. Miramon (1972)—reasonably likely to render and rendering reasonably effective assistance. See also United States v. Butler (1974)—reasonbly competent assistance—and Moore v. United States (1970).

13. People v. Heirens (1954).

14. *Id.* at 140, 122 N.E.2d at 237. Defense counsel further stated: "I have no memory of any case, certainly not in my time at the bar, when counsel on both sides were so perplexed as to the mental status of an individual and the causes which motivated him to do certain acts.'" *Id.* at 130, 122 N.E.2d at 236.

15. Quoted in *id.* at 140, 122 N.E.2d at 237.

16. *Id.* at 140, 122 N.E.2d at 236.

17. 122 N.E.2d at 236.

18. Professor Alschuler (1968) has observed with respect to the case: "[Defendant's] culpability under the traditional legal standards was doubtful, yet both the defendant and society were deprived of an authoritative resolution of this issue. [Defendant] is today an inmate of the Stateville Penitentiary although no one has determined on the basis of the evidence that a prison is where he belongs. Society devised the insanity defense precisely to avoid such distressing spectacles."

19. Compare, e.g., Curits (1951) with Drinker (1952); Burger (1966) with Freedman (1966); Frankel (1975) with Freedman (1975).

REFERENCES

ALSCHULER, A. (1968). "The prosecutor's role in plea bargaining." University of Chicago Law Review, 36:50, 75.

American Bar Association Journal (1958). Professional responsibility: Report of the joint conference." 44:1159, 1161, 1162.

BAZELON, D. (1973). "The defective assistance of counsel." University of Cincinnati Law Review, 42:1, 28.

BRESS, D. (1966). "Standards of conduct of the prosecution and defense function: An attorney's viewpoint." American Criminal Law Quarterly, 5:23, 24-25.

BROWN v. SWENSON (1973). 8th Cir. 506 F.2d 1236, 1240, cert. denied. (1975) 420 U.S. 978.

BURGER, W. (1966). "Standards of conduct for prosecution and defense personnel: A judge's viewpoint." American Criminal Law Quarterly, 5:11, 15.

CARLIN, J. and HOWARD, J. (1965). "Legal representation and class justice." UCLA Law Review, 12:381.

CURTIS, C. (1951). "The ethics of advocacy." Stanford Law Review, 4:3, 12.

Davis v. Bomar (1965). 6th Cir. 344 F.2d 84, 89, cert. denied (1965). 383 U.S. 883.

DRINKER, H. (1952). "Some remarks on Mr. Curtis' 'the ethics of advocacy'." Stanford Law Review, 4:349.

FRANKEL, M. (1975). "The search for truth: An umpireal view." University of Pennsylvania Law Review, 123:1031, 1057-1058.

FREEDMAN, M. (1966). "Professional responsibility of the criminal defense lawyer: The three hardest questions." Michigan Law Review, 64:1469, 1482.

——— (1967). "The professional responsibility of the prosecuting attorney." Georgetown Law Journal, 55:1030.

——— (1975). "Judge Frankel's search for truth." University of Pennsylvania Law Review, 123:1060, 1065.

FULLER, L. (1961). "The adversary system." Pp. 30, 37 in Berman (ed.), Talks on American law. New York: Random.

Hayes v. Russell (1969). 6th Cir. 405 F.2d 859, 860.

Herring v. Estelle (1974). 5th Cir. 491 F.2d 125, 128.

Moore v. United States (1970). 3d Cir. 432 F.2d 730, 736.

NOONAN, T. (1966). "The purposes of advocacy and the limits of confidentiality." Michigan Law Review, 64:1485, 1487.

People v. Belge (1975). Onondaga County Court. 83 Misc. 2d 186, 372 N.Y.S.2d 798.

People v. Heirens (1954). 4 Ill. 2d 131, 122 N.E. 2d, cert. denied (1955). 349 U.S. 947.

United States v. Butler (1974). D.C. Cir. 504 F.2d 220, 223.

United States v. Miramon (1972). 9th Cir. 470 F.2d 1362, 1363, cert. denied (1973). 411 U.S. 934.

United States v. Sanchez (1973). 2d Cir. 483 F.2d 1052, 1057, cert. denied (1974). 415 U.S. 991.

Yale Law Journal (1970). "Legal ethics and professionalism." 79:1179, 1186, 1189.

Robert M. Regoli
Texas Christian University

5

STUDYING DISCREPANCIES BETWEEN POLICE-CITIZEN ANOMIA LEVELS

The police are but one element in the system of criminal control, but their visibility so greatly exceeds that of other elements such as prosecutors, judges, and correctional workers, that for most citizens police are their only contact with the system and therefore the primary symbolic representation of it. This heightens their importance, since experiences with police prompt citizens to generalize the same impressions to other elements of the system. Many of these impressions derive from attitudes and values of police, which are likely to be revealed overtly or covertly during police-citizen encounters.

Previous research has demonstrated that police do have distinctive attitudes and values:

> He can develop a somewhat paranoid outlook in his social perceptions, with a tendency to assign evil intentions to others. Society can come to be viewed as a vicious "dog eat dog" jungle, in which only force can insure peace and harmony. [Toch, 1973: 89]

> The policeman is a cynic. Faced with the duty of keeping the people in line, and believing that most people are out to break the law and do him harm if possible, he always looks for the selfish motive. [Westley, 1970: 147]

> If the officer feels estranged, disregarded except upon command and unimportant when it counts, the mask of distrust, cynicism, and ultimately, brutality may fit more easily . . . Worn long enough, the mask fuses with the face. [Chwast, 1970: 118]

Generally, researchers believe the reason police hold distinctive attitudes and values is because of unusual occupational demands facing them. Even among writers basing their conclusions on subjective, rather than objective measures, the "occupational demands" variable becomes crucial when explaining police officer attitudes and values. For example,

> . . . The story is all coppers are just civilians like anyone else, living among them not in barracks like on the Continent, but you and I know that's just a legend for mugs. We are cut off: we're not like everyone else. Some civilians fear us and play up to us, some dislike us and keep out of our way, but no one—well, very few indeed—accepts us as just ordinary like them. In one sense, dear, we're just like hostile troops occupying an enemy country. And say what you like, at times it makes us lonely. [MacInnes, 1962: 20]

The implication from this and other writings is clear. If the "occupational demands" variable were neutralized, it is hypothesized, then police and citizens would show similar attitude and value patterns. Thus, police are people who, once they choose their occupation, have little control over how various attitudes and values would develop. Further, the implication from research is that once an individual enters the police occupation, his attitudes will change negatively. It is not uncommon to hear charges of police being insensitive, authoritarian, cynical, alienated, dogmatic, or even anomic—how else are high rates of suicide among police accounted for?

This paper focuses on explaining police-citizen attitude differences from a different angle. The basis for the project stems from a Denver study where the degree of anomia among police and citizen groups was examined (Bayley and Mendelsohn, 1968). The conclusion reached by these researchers was that "Denver police consistently scored lower on the anomia scale than the Dominant general public" (Bayley and Mendelsohn, 1968:15-16). But unfortunately the researchers stopped there. They did not go on to give an explanation of why police might score lower on an anomia index. Needless to say, these results were contradictory to what was expected. Thus, the researchers would have had difficulty attaching any traditional theoretical orientation to these unexpected findings.

But in 1973, a book appeared which focused on a previously unappreciated topic in American criminological theory. That book, *The New Criminology* (Taylor, Walton, and Young, 1973), was the first comprehensive effort toward developing a critical philosophy of justice, one which would have aided Bayley and Mendelsohn (1968) in explaining their results. Taylor, Walton, and Young's work, and those following it, have become labeled as "radical criminology." The tenets of this theoretical orientation are outlined in Quinney's *Critique of Legal Order* (1974:15-16):

> Although the legal order consists of more than criminal law, criminal law is the foundation of that order. It is the coercive instrument of the state, used by the state and its ruling class to maintain the existing social and economic order. A critical theory of crime control in American society can be outlined systematically as follows:
>
> 1. American society is based on an advanced capitalist society.
> 2. The state is organized to serve the interests of the dominant economic class . . . .
> 3. Criminal law is an instrument of the state and ruling class to maintain and perpetuate the existing social and economic order.
> 4. Crime control in capitalist society is accomplished through a variety of institutions and agencies established and administered by a governmental elite . . .
> 5. The contradictions of advanced capitalism . . . require that the subordinate classes remain oppressed by whatever means necessary . . .

6. Only with the collapse of capitalist society and the creation of a new society . . . will there be a solution to the crime problem.

To maintain this privileged position, the "ruling elite" rely on two specific institutions of social control: police (at home) and military (abroad). When discussing the recommendations of the President's Crime Commission for police, Quinney notes (1974:175):

> Rather than questioning the existence of the law enforcement institution in the capitalist state, most social scientists offer measures that would strengthen the police and increase their ability to perform . . . What is actually being advocated is further manipulation of the public consciousness so that the police can more effectively fulfill their function of preserving domestic order . . . What we are not offered . . . is a change that would get to the basis of criminal justice in a capitalist society.

Thus, because police are an arm of the "ruling elite," they are granted privileges unknown to "common" citizens. Consequently, even though police face unusual occupational demands, this does not necessarily lead to the formation of negative attitudes, specifically, anomia. Rather, the converse, based on "radical" criminology tenets, is hypothesized. Because police are granted special privileges (in carrying out the mission of the "ruling elite") they become insulated against anomia producing conditions. It is hypothesized that:

> Police will be significantly less anomic than citizen groups.

Research Design

To test the hypothesis that police will be less anomic than citizens they serve, two independent samples were selected. One came from a survey of 222 patrolmen, representing nine law enforcement agencies, during the summer of 1973; in no case was less than 70% of an agency sampled (all patrolmen were white males). Thus, it is safe to assume these officers represent attitudes across their departments. The second sample came from the 1974 NORC study, where 1,484 resondents were interviewed. But because all police sampled were male, only males from the NORC data were utilized in the analysis. Thus, 691 of 1,484 respondents were applicable.

To measure anomia all respondents were asked to complete Srole's (1956) anomia index (see Appendix 1). According to Srole (1956), *anomia is perceived as an individual's generalized, pervasive sense of malintegration*. The scale consists of five items, each measuring one aspect of anomia. Responses to each item are either "agree," "disagree," or "undecided," with one point given to an "agree" response; the other responses warranted zero points.

In the present research, this procedure was modified slightly. Instead of scoring each item either 1 or 0, each item was scored either 2 (for a "disagree" or "undecided" response) or 4 (for an "agree" response); scores ranged from 10-20; with high scores indicating greater anomia manifested by the respondent.

For statistical purposes, respondents were dichotomized into high and low subgroupings. Respondents having an anomia index composite score equal to or greater than 15 were classified as highly anomic; all others were considered low anomics. Because independent samples are being contrasted, statistical analysis is restricted to descriptive measures.

Table 1. PERCENTAGE OF POPULATION CATEGORIZED AS HIGHLY ANOMIC

Item	Northwest Police (N = 222)	Citizens (N = 691)
Srole 1	37.39	58.32
Srole 2	9.91	39.51
Srole 3	36.04	49.49
Srole 4	8.11	32.42
Srole 5	43.24	30.82
Srole Total	24.32	39.94

Results

If the radical criminology perspective is correct, then police will show less anomia than citizens. To test this, the samples were compared on the anomia index. As shown in Table 1, the percentage of police scoring high on the anomia index is much less than that reported among citizens. Overall, 24% of the police, as compared to 40% of the citizens scored highly anomic. Further, this difference appears for four of the five anomia items.

Next the data were analyzed controlling for race. To do this, the NORC data were dichotomized into white and nonwhite citizens and these groups were compared to the police sample. The results from this procedure are shown in Table 2. Here it is noted that the white population has

Table 2. PERCENTAGE OF POPULATION CATEGORIZED AS HIGHLY ANOMIC CONTROLLING FOR RACE

Item	Northwest Police (N = 222)	Whites (N = 619)	Nonwhites (N = 72)
Srole 1	37.39	60.90	36.11
Srole 2	9.91	41.52	22.22
Srole 3	36.04	49.76	47.22
Srole 4	8.11	33.60	22.22
Srole 5	43.32	28.92	6.94
Srole Total	24.32	42.81	15.28

a considerably higher proportion of their members in the highly anomic category than either the police or nonwhites have. In fact, 43% of the whites scored highly anomic while only 15% of the nonwhites were placed in the highly anomic group. This finding remained relatively consistent for each of the Srole items.

Because this finding is contradictory to existing literature (especially strain theory), analysis was carried an additional step controlling for respondent's educational level and race simultaneously. To do this, respondents were dichotomized into high (over 14 years of education) and low (14 and less years of education) subgroups. The results from this procedure proved enlightening. As Table 3 shows, among police the effects of controlling for educational level were negligible. Among less educated police, 26% were highly

Table 3. PERCENTAGE OF POPULATION CATEGORIZED AS HIGHLY ANOMIC CONTROLLING FOR EDUCATION LEVEL AND RACE

	Northwest Police		Whites		Nonwhites	
Item	LE (143)	HE (79)	LE (483)	HE (134)	LE (66)	HE (7)
Srole 1	37.06	37.97	56.52	77.61	36.36	NA
Srole 2	10.49	8.86	38.10	56.72	30.30	NA
Srole 3	40.56	27.85	59.42	89.55	42.42	NA
Srole 4	9.09	6.33	28.36	52.99	21.21	NA
Srole 5	44.76	40.51	22.98	47.76	7.59	NA
Srole Total	25.87	21.52	35.61	69.40	16.67	NA

LE: low education; HE: high education; NA: not applicable

anomic; among the more educated police 22% were. But among white citizens, the differences are pronounced. Thirty-six percent of less educated whites were highly anomic, while among more educated whites, 69% were. Among less educated nonwhites, only 17% scored in the highly anomic group.

Next, differences between groups were examined controlling for social class and race simultaneously. To measure social class, respondents were placed into either low or middle class subgroups (depending on their responses to questionnaire and interview items). Table 4 shows that low and middle class police are about equally likely to be highly anomic (25.37% versus 23.87%). But among citizens, Table 4 shows that middle class whites are considerably more likely than lower class whites to fall in the highly anomic category (48% versus 27%).

Table 4. PERCENTAGE OF POPULATION CATEGORIZED AS HIGHLY ANOMIC CONTROLLING FOR SOCIAL CLASS AND RACE

	Northwest Police		Whites		Nonwhites	
Item	Low (67)	Middle (155)	Low (323)	Middle (296)	Low (49)	Middle (23)
Srole 1	29.85	40.65	53.25	69.59	32.65	43.48
Srole 2	11.94	9.03	31.27	52.70	26.53	13.04
Srole 3	29.85	38.71	56.97	75.68	53.06	34.78
Srole 4	4.48	9.68	26.01	42.23	22.45	21.74
Srole 5	44.78	42.58	21.36	35.81	6.12	8.70
Srole Total	25.37	23.87	26.62	48.30	16.33	13.04

Another interesting note is that when controlling for either race or social class, *all* white subgroups had a higher percentage of their members placed in the highly anomic category than either nonwhites or police. Among nonwhite citizens, class makes little difference. Among lower class nonwhites, 16% placed in the highly anomic group, while 13% of the middle class nonwhites were so placed.

Finally, the analysis was redone holding race, educational level, and social class constant simultaneously. The results are shown in Table 5. Because of insufficient cell sizes, two subgroups were eliminated (lower class educated nonwhites and middle class educated nonwhites). When controlling for these variables, the results are noteworthy. First, among police, those who are educated and in the lower class have the greatest percentage of members scoring highly anomic. Second, among whites, the group having the highest percentage of anomics is the educated, middle class subcategory (nearly 70%), followed by educated, lower class respondents (54%) while the remaining subgroups had considerably lower percentages, of their members in this category. Among nonwhites, the lower class, less educated respondents had a larger proportion of their members in the highly anomic category than did the middle class, less educated nonwhites, but the difference was negligible (16% versus 9%).

CONCLUSION AND IMPLICATIONS

The difficulty is now providing an explanation for unexpected results. If we tried to fit our results to a "strain" theory model, we would find ourselves arguing that the group with the highest percentage of anomics suffers from the least economic strain. Such an explanation would not be entirely unreasonable if we relied on Durkheim's conception of anomie as opposed to Merton's. But what would be necessary is to show that middle class, educated whites

Table 5. PERCENTAGE OF POPULATIONS CATEGORIZED AS HIGHLY ANOMIC CONTROLLING FOR RACE, CLASS, AND EDUCATION

	Northwest Police (N = 222)				Whites (N = 619)				Nonwhites (N = 72)			
	Low (N = 67)		Middle (N = 155)		Low (N = 323)		Middle (N = 296)		Low (N = 49)		Middle (N = 23)	
Item	LE (43)	HE (24)	LE (100)	HE (55)	LE (295)	HE (26)	LE (188)	HE (108)	LE (44)	HE (5)	LE (22)	HE (1)
Srole 1	27.91	33.33	41.00	40.00	51.19	76.92	64.36	77.78	31.82	NA	45.45	NA
Srole 2	11.63	12.50	10.00	7.25	30.51	42.31	45.74	64.81	27.27	NA	13.64	NA
Srole 3	27.91	33.33	47.00	25.45	54.92	80.77	66.49	91.96	47.73	NA	31.64	NA
Srole 4	2.33	8.33	12.00	5.45	24.41	46.15	34.04	54.63	22.73	NA	18.18	NA
Srole 5	39.53	54.17	47.00	34.55	19.32	46.15	28.72	48.15	6.82	NA	9.09	NA
Srole Total	18.60	37.50	29.00	14.55	29.15	53.85	45.74	69.74	16.32	NA	9.09	NA

LE: low education
HE: high education
NA: not applicable

experienced tragedy or fortune immediately preceding the survey, and there is no evidence that either kind of event occurred. But "strain" theory is not alone in its difficulty to account for the results. In fact, nearly all contemporary theories would have difficulty. The reason for this is clear. To quote Quinney (1974:1):

> We do not adequately understand our contemporary existence. Our comprehension obscured by our current consciousness—a consciousness developed within the existing order and serving only to maintain that order. If we are ever to remove the oppression of the age, we must critically understand the world about us . . . Nowhere is the inadequacy of our understanding more apparent than in our thoughts and actions in relation to legal order.

Essentially then, Quiney (1974) argues that the primary reason contemporary explanations of deviance (including police misconduct) are inadequate is because they all confirm an official ideology—one supporting existing social and economic institutions.

The condition in the present paper is similar. Because all previous theories were developed to confirm a capitalistic model, then it should not be surprising they have difficulty accounting for data not fitting that model. Thus, to explain the data, it is necessary to turn toward a critical philosophy.

A most interesting finding is that few nonwhites are highly anomic. This implies that these people are content with their position in the social order. Further, the finding indicates that the capitalistic system has been successful in conditioning them to accept a "station-in-life." There are various mechanisms by which the existing order has established control over these people. One is juvenile correctional institutions (Liazos, 1974:2):

> . . . I believe it is because it has never been the intent of any of these programs to change the conditions that consign poor and working class youths to menial, dead-end jobs and

> condemn to the juvenile justice system those who refuse to (or cannot) fit into this mold. All the programs through the years have aimed at control and discipline of the poorer classes; they have tried to resocialize the boys and girls of the poor, working class, and minority groups so that they would accept the place capitalism (in its various forms) chose for them.

But why the high percentage of anomics among the middle class white groups? Again, the explanation is similar. The "system" has been able to generate a belief among these people that they need to strive for rewards the system produces. Thus, these people appear highly anomic because they are striving for the "American myth"; that is, status within existing social and economic institutions. Because the existing order can only stand a limited amount of mobility, only a few from the middle class can succeed. The remainder continue to struggle upward, becoming frustrated, often disenchanted, and anomic.

But the system, apparently is successful in defining a "station-in-life" for these people also. As long as these individuals' energy is directed toward fulfilling prescribed desires, the existing order should remain stable. But the data do suggest that this group is becoming highly intolerant to a restrictive order, thus, high anomia results. If the radical criminology perspective is correct, one would suspect that as anomia becomes increasingly prevalent this group will become instrumental in social change. But, both the form or when that change will occur are unanswered in the data.

The most significant finding of these data shows the police having a considerably lower percentage of their members scoring highly anomic than whites. Adopting a radical criminology perspective, the reason is obvious. Police are people in our society being granted a "special status" by the ruling elite. Police are individuals who have been given authority to enforce laws, kill, or almost anything else necessary to preserve existing social and economic institutions. Simply, police officers are the subjects of the "ruling elite." Consequently, police are ordinary people who are allowed to change roles. That is, during their working day, police experience the role of "oppressor," while off duty, they become one of the "oppressed." There is no doubt that when police are performing their "special functions" they are above the law. To quote Krisberg (1975: 13-14):

> . . . we need to understand the distinction between distributive justice and social justice. If the police officer who killed the alleged car thief were to be tried and convicted, this would be an example of distributive justice, in that the policeman would not have received special treatment by the courts. But the pursuit of social justice requires that one consider the reasons why the police officer resorted to deadly force . . . The judge who tells us that the officer was only "doing his duty" tells us that the policeman's duty is first and foremost to protect private property.

Thus, police can be conceptualized as a group in an occupation making unusual demands upon them. But these demands do not necessarily lead to negative attributes as previous research has argued. Rather, it is argued here that the "special rights" police receive far outweigh negative consequences coming from demands placed on them. Thus, because of their special status position, police are isolated from many of the frustrations facing "common whites." Consequently, it was predicted and noted that the percentage of anomics among police would be fewer than among whites generally.

Finally, what do the data imply? First, the data show the need for capitalistic societies to establish control over its members. Further, the data indicate that the capitalistic order in the United States is functioning successfully in establishing control over each segment of its population. Briefly, nonwhites appear content while whites are struggling to achieve more for themselves within the existing framework without questioning it. Apparently the system has convinced people that it is providing for them, including their wishes and desires, rather than revealing its latent goal of exploitation and dominance. Finally, the data show that occupational demands made on individual police serve to insulate them against frustrations generated by the capitalistic systems need to maintain control.

REFERENCES

BAYLEY, D. and MENDELSOHN, H. (1968). Minorities and the police: Confrontation in America. New York: Free Press.

CHWAST, J. (1970). "Value conflicts in law enforcement." Pp. 113-119 in A. Niederhoffer and A. Blumberg (eds.), The ambivalent force. Walthan, MA: Xerox Publishing.

KRISBERG, B. (1975). Crime and privilege. Englewood Cliffs, NJ: Prentice-Hall.

LIAZOS, A. (1974). "Class opression: The functions of juvenile justice." Insurgent Sociologist, 1 (fall):2-24.

MACINNES, C. (1962). Mr. Love and justice. London: New England Library.

QUINNEY, R. (1974). Critique of legal order. New York: Little, Brown.

ROKEACH, M. et al. (1971). "The value gap between police and policed." Journal of Social Issues, 27(2):155-171.

SROLE, L. (1956). "Social integration and certain corollaries." American Sociological Review, 21(6):709-716.

TAYLOR, I., WALTON, P., and YOUNG, J. (1973). The new criminology. New York: Harper Torchbooks.

TOCH, H. (1973). "Psychological consequences of the police role." Pp. 85-92 in E. Eldefonso (ed.), Readings in criminal justice. New York: Glencoe Press.

WESTLEY, W. (1970). Violence and the police. Cambridge, Mass: MIT Press.

APPENDIX:
Srole (1956) Anomia Scale

Anomia is viewed as an individual's generalized, pervasive sense of social malintegration or "self-to-others alienation" (versus self-to-other's belongingness).

Anomia Items

(1) There's little use writing to public officials because they often aren't really interested in the problems of the average man.

(2) Nowadays a person has to live pretty much for today and let tomorrow take care of itself.

(3) In spite of what some people say, the lot of the average man is getting worse, not better.

(4) It's hardly fair to bring children into the world with the way things look for the future.

(5) These days a person doesn't really know whom he can count on.

SOURCE: Srole (1956:21, 709-716).

Carol Bohmer
Rutgers Law School

6

PSYCHIATRISTS AND PRESENTENCE REPORTS: A Case of Role Stress

The criminal law is a man-made system proscribing certain kinds of behavior among members of a society. If a member behaves in a proscribed way he is brought before the court, part of the system, to prove whether in fact he has violated a rule. The judge, either by himself or with a jury, operates through appropriate procedural rules to determine whether the offender has committed the act of which he has been charged. It is then for the judge, the duly appointed official, to decide how best to express society's disapprobation of the offender's activities and to deter him from further infractions of the criminal law.

The law sets down certain basic guidelines within which the judge must operate in making such decisions. Each particular offense for which the offender has been convicted has set down for it maximum, and sometimes minimum, possible prison sentences. In certain situations, the judge has available to him probation, and also a sentence longer than the specified maximum, as when an offender can be classified as an "habitual offender," a "criminal psychopath," or a "sexual psychopath," within appropriate legislative definitions.

Within these limits, which are in fact very broad, a judge usually has wide discretion to pass whatever sentence he thinks best in the circumstances. It is clear that the judge has been given such wide discretion because he is able to insert a human personal element into what is an incredibly weighty responsibility; that is, to decide what should be the course of a man's life and often for a large part of that life. While this personal element may result in inconsistent, arbitrary, or irrational sentencing decisions, it is the judge's feelings and intuitions that are considered to be the life of the law and therefore desirable.

The judge's decision in sentencing may be influenced by three sets of factors:

(1) his personal views and philosophy;
(2) external pressures; and
(3) formal advice.

It is this third factor, that of formal advice, which is the major focus of this paper. Given the movement toward rehabilitation and individualization of sentencing it is considered vital that the judge be provided with the maximum possible information on which to base his decision. It is to fulfill the need for background information that presentence probation reports are provided to the judge at his request, or if required by legislation. More recently, as part of a general increase in the role of psychiatry in the legal system, some courts have access to psychiatric clinics, one major function of which is to prepare psychiatric presentence reports as a further sentencing aid for the judge. It is usually within the discretion of the judge to determine those cases for which he can be assisted by psychiatric reports.

This paper is intended to examine this psychiatric presentence report and its implications. How does the psychiatrist fit into the picture? What is his role as evaluator of the defendant for the purpose of preparing a report? How does this role fit into accepted objectives and procedures of psychiatry? What is the defendant's interest in this process? To what legal protection is he entitled?

The Psychiatric Clinic and the Court Psychiatrist

Psychiatric court clinics, which generally exist only in metropolitan centers, vary somewhat in their organization and function. Several of them have been described in detail elsewhere, so that discussion will be limited to those salient points relevant to this paper.[1]

One major focus of the clinic is the evaluation of convicted offenders prior to their sentencing. This evaluation usually culminates in a written report, which discusses the defendant's psychiatric and social history, his current mental status, a diagnosis of any psychiatric abnormality, some explanation of the behavior which led him to court, and a prediciton about future behavior. The reports frequently include recommendations by the psychiatrists in their advisory capacities as to the most suitable legal and psychiatric dispositions of offenders. These recommendations and the reports wherein they are contained are considered to be one of the most important pieces of data used by the judge in making sentencing decisions.[2]

The above discussion should make it abundantly clear that court clinic psychiatrists perform very different tasks from those of their colleagues in private practice or in psychiatric hospitals. The court psychiatrist is a clinician serving as an advisor and evaluator in a circumscribed situation and as such is unlikely to have any opportunity to conduct follow-up investigations of the outcome of the cases. They may, but by accident rather than design, see some of their "mistakes" when offenders commit additional crimes and are sent to the court clinic for reevaluation.

The psychiatrist may be seen as in fact having two "clients": the offender and the judge. Problems of role conflict may arise here in the different pressures felt by the psychiatrist in carrying out his duties to each "client." The orientation of a psychiatrist is toward (a) helping individuals; (b) generally helping only willing patients; and (c) the development of a private, personal, and confidential relationship with his client. The evaluation of an unwilling offender with whom the psychiatrist has no further contact and about whom he writes a report to be read by a third party tends to violate all of the above elements of the psychiatrist's orientation. The report written for the judge may advocate a disposition which, while it may be paternalistically seen to be "in the best interests of the offender," may be far from an ideal disposition in the eyes of the offender.

The psychiatrist is providing a service for the court and not for the patient. Court psychiatrists have been quick to point out that they work as *consultants* to the judge. They also emphasize their independence in relation to the attorneys in the case. Said one in an interview, "We are independent professionals, not agents of the prosecution." Another court psychiatrist said that he felt he was working for the judge, not the district attorney or the defense. The term "friend of the court" was also used to describe the psychiatrist's role as one removed from the adversary process. This is clearly one way of viewing one's role (accurate or not). Another view was taken by the psychiatrist who considered that he was working for himself, and dismissed suggestions of any allegiance to anyone in the system.[3]

The court psychiatrist may feel impotent in his desire to help the individuals whom he sees and he may feel that he is not appropriately fulfilling this professional role. It may be a need to do more than this which prompts some of the psychiatrists to extend beyond their limited function of individual evaluation in the preparation of reports. Sometimes the psychiatrist's training and orientation becomes overpowering and he makes efforts to treat the defendant during the evaluation. As one psychiatrist put it, "I enjoy talking to people. I am the slowest interviewer here. I like to give them a feeling of what treating is all about—I do treating when I am talking to them." And another, "The inverviews are a sort of one-shot treatment, like a friend or relative." This view of treatment and the conditions under which it is conducted is not one with which many psychiatrists would agree. Indeed, another psychiatrist in the court clinic not only does not see what he is doing as having anything to do with treatment, but is in fact glad to be relieved of the task of treating the defendants he sees in the clinic. He said, "I have no responsibility to see the person after. I would be pretty frustrated if I would have to treat the people I see here."

The expansion of the psychiatric role from that of merely evaluating to something broader or perhaps more closely related to the psychiatric role in private practice can also be seen in such matters as the recommendations made. For example, when questioned in an interview as to why the psychiatrist made a recommendation advocating that the offender be sent to a type of facility that did not exist, he responded that he was thereby indicating to the judge the need for such facilities. He perceives himself as fulfilling an additional function, that of unofficial lobbyist for changes in the available facilities. The problem with taking on such a function is that it may be misinterpreted by the judge, who may simply think that the psychiatrist is unfamiliar with available facilities.

A further problem experienced by the court psychiatrist is the extent to which he is subject to the judge's criticism. A classic problem faced by many professionals is the laymen's belief that he is competent to pass judgment on the subject. This problem is especially pronounced for the court psychiatrist, who may be criticized and even advised as to how to write reports by the judge. The judge, to whom in a sense the psychiatrist is reponsible, comments on what he considers the competence, or lack thereof, of the psychiatrist. For example, on several occasions in interviews, judges mentioned the background data included in the reports, as well as the psychiatrist's sociological explanation of the etiology of the crime.[4] Thus, a judge would ask rhetorical questions, such as the following: "Why does he bother to tell me the man comes from a ghetto?" "What do *they* know about it?" "What good does it do me to know that this fellow has led a disorganized life?" The judges were commenting on those parts of the report which they considered unhelpful and superfluous, and which in addition they considered the psychiatrist unqualified to make. In a sense the judges were criticizing what they saw as the psychiatrist's overstepping the boundary of his expertise (Greenwood, 1971:3-16). However, there is a difference in perception of professional role here. For the psychiatrist, such "background data" are considered a crucial part of his evaluation and therefore an appropriate area of discussion in his report.

It is apparent that the psychiatrists who work in court clinics must cope with their role conflicts and role ambiguities in some way that is satisfactory to them. However, from an objective point of view, a professional who works in a bureaucracy (here the court system) is inevitably bound by different rules and loyalties than are his colleagues in private practice. As Szasz (1965:56) puts it,

> In a medical situation it is not enough to note who is the doctor and who the recipient of his medical attention. The latter is not necessarily a "patient" nor the former a "physician"—at least not in the usual sense of these terms. Whenever the physician is employed by someone other than the patient, his loyalty and responsibility to his employer must be frankly recognized. In some cases such loyalty to third parties does not interfere with the physician's conscientious care of sick persons. In others it interferes only slightly. In still others, it requires that the "patient" be harmed rather than helped.

Thus the professional in a bureaucracy may find that the goals of his professional conflict with those of the organization. More specifically, as Szasz points out, despite all the protestations of independence quoted above, the psychiatrist may be required by his allegiance to the institution to harm the "patient," something which is quite alien to the role of medical doctor.

In the court clinic situation, there appears to be a lack of clear definition of who is the client. If it is the offender who is the client, he has no control over "his" psychiatrist at all, unlike the psychiatrist's client in private practice, who has the ultimate control, the power to discontinue his role as client. The offender's only right in this situation is to refuse to speak to the psychiatrist, an action which is very likely to tell against him at sentencing, for he will have shown himself to be uncooperative and may therefore be treated more harshly. In interviews, court clinic psychiatrists varied in their responses to questions about how they would handle a defendant who refused to speak to them. One simply said that he would send the offender back to court without trying to persuade him to speak. Another, however, puts pressure on defendants in such cases. He tells them, "If you don't want to talk to us, you are in contempt of court, and we will send you for observation for sixty days, and if they can't learn about you from your behavior, off you go to Fairview."

The fact that the defendant is often not the psychiatrist's client in the true sense of the word may be made clear by some psychiatrists, both in the court clinic or in situations where a defendant is being examined by the psychiatrist hired by the other side. For example, some psychiatrists hired by the prosecution are careful to point out that they are not there to help the defendants, and that they should accordingly be aware of the psychiatrists' enemy status. However, the extent of such practice is open to question, especially if the psychiatrist feels, as many do, that taking an adversative stance will interfere with the rapport needed to conduct an adequate psychiatric interview.

In the court clinic interview, some defendants may already know (or have guessed) that the court psychiatrist is *not* a friend. As one psychiatrist put it, "Some of them know what I am doing, through having been in the system. They look on me as a punitive figure who can harm them in some way and help them in some way." Again there is some variation in the way the court psychiatrists handle this situation. Some are careful to explain their role to the defendant, while others are content to let whatever assumptions are made stand as they are. Said one, "We don't tell them who we are unless they appear to be confused. We make sure that they know we are not the enemy. Sometimes we turn out to be the enemy."

If the offender can afford it—which most offenders cannot—he can engage his own psychiatrist who can present a report on his behalf to the court. However, although the defendant here is truly the psychiatrist's client, the report is not the official court-ordered report and will not therefore have the same status as that of the court psychiatrist.

Confidentiality and Privilege

Of major concern to the psychiatric profession are the two related issues of psychiatric confidentiality and privilege. It is felt that unless psychiatrists gain and keep the confidence of their patients they are not able to successfuly fulfill their professional role. To keep this confidence, the patient must trust his therapist to act solely in the patient's interest and for his benefit. The psychiatrist must accordingly not reveal information about the patient or the therapy to anyone else. Because verbal communication is the major tool of the psychiatrist, this trust is particularly important, for without such trust the patient will be less likely to reveal important material and the therapist less likely to be able to help.

Organizations which represent the psychiatric profession, such as the American Psychiatric Association and the Group for the Advancement of Psychiatry, have frequently made public statements outlining the positions of the organizations on such issues. They are viewed in part as ethical issues and therefore matters of the utmost importance to the reputation of the psychiatric profession (e.g., American Psychiatric Association, 1973:1057).

Confidentiality and privilege are two different but related concepts.[6] Confidentiality, whereby the psychiatrist is bound to keep secret confidences entrusted to him during the course of therapy, is based on the patient's right to privacy, as well as his contractual right to his therapist's silence. Privilege, on the other hand, is the legal right of the patient established by statute in many states not to have information revealed in court by his doctor.

Many psychiatrists are concerned that the concepts of confidentiality and privilege are too broad to adequately protect their special relationships with their patients. They fear that third parties, particularly legislatures and courts, do not understand just how crucial privacy is to the psychiatrist-patient relationship.

> In psychiatry, where it is the very essence of the patient's personal life, security from abuses of privacy form a condition without which it would be difficult to practice psychiatry and psychotherapy at all. [American Psychiatric Association, 1975:iv]

Nowhere, admist all of the ethical and practical concern by psychiatrists for the best way of practicing their profession and protecting their patients, is mention ever made about the area discussed in this paper. The rights of defendants interviewed for the purpose of preparing a presentence report are never mentioned. Let it also be remembered that the defendant is not always informed of the true nature of his relationship with the psychiatrist.

Psychiatrists may not consider this a relationship in which confidentiality is necessary, since it is not one in which a therapeutic relationship is being built up. However, given the expressed reluctance of many psychiatrists to inform defendants of their adversary role because of their fear of spoiling necessary rapport, the argument that no trust need be developed and therefore no confidentiality protected seems hollow. It is very odd, particularly in the light of the extensive literature in this area in general, that this aspect of the psychiatric role goes unmentioned. How is it that a psychiatrist can so readily set aside his emphasis on trust and confidentiality simply by changing the word patient to defendant?

Confidentiality is in fact mentioned in the literature about psychiatric presentence reports, but in a very different context from that discussed above. The term confidentiality in this context in no way involves the right to privacy of the defendant:

> The confidentiality of a presentence investigation report of a probation department, diagnostic center, or court probation clinic is a matter which is receiving increased attention. . . . The issue here is not the right of the defendant to have information withheld from the court but rather of the court to withhold information from the convicted defendant or his attorney. [Slovenko, 1966:126]

No elaboration or explanation is given for this reversal of the meaning.

The patient-therapist privilege is also a matter of great concern for psychiatrists. In a recent case, a psychiatrist refused to testify in court about therapy undergone 10 years prior to the suit, and was cited for contempt of court (In re Lifschutz, 1970). The psychiatrist was lauded as a hero in the press and in psychiatric literature for his courageous action in attempting to broaden the psychiatrist-patient privilege and in emphasizing the vital need for such a privilege.

Again, privilege, as it might apply to defendants being evaluated for psychiatric reports, is not mentioned in the literature. Such court-ordered examinations generally fall within the statutory exceptions to the privilege, presumably because this is an area where other interests are considered more important; for example, the need of the court to the maximum information for sentencing. While understandable, legally this is, of course, a radical change for the psychiatrist whose role is no longer protector of the interests of the patient, but protector of the interests of society.

Disclosure of the Psychiatric Report

Jurisdictions vary in their approach to disclosure of presentence reports. The practice in Philadelphia is that the psychiatric report is disclosed to the judge, the defense attorney, and the district attorney, although there is no legal requirement that this be done. In a few jurisdictions, there is a requirement that the probation presentence report be disclosed to the defendant.[7] On the whole, however, the matter frequently is left to the sentencing judge's discretion. There has been considerable discussion as to whether the defendant does or should have a *right* to access to the probation presentence report.[8] On the one hand it is argued that anything less than the maximum sentence is a privilege and therefore the defendant has no right to see the report, which is in part the basis for the decision.

Constitutional arguments have been considered not to apply since the sentencing report is written after conviction: "[A]fter conviction a case ceases to be an action at law and becomes a social problem" (Hincks, 1944:7). On the other hand, many scholars agree that sentencing is a vital part of the criminal process and therefore should be conducted in accordance with due process. The argument in favor of disclosure of the presentence report is related to the defendant's right to a hearing on sentencing which should be represented by counsel and given an opportunity to rebut information contained in the probation report. Some of the arguments made in favor of or against mandatory disclosure apply also to psychiatric presentence reports. However, there are special issues which arise out of the very different nature of the information gathering process as well as the content of the two types of presentence reports.

Much of the case law on the question of disclosure of the probation presentence report arises out of fact situations in which it is shown that the sentencing judge relied on certain facts which are shown to be inaccurate. By contrast much of the data included in a psychiatric presentence report is nonspecific and difficult to rebut. It is not information but rather the diagnostic impressions and opinions of the examining psychiatrist and therefore can only be rebutted by other expert psychiatric opinion. Much has been written about the "unscientific" nature of psychiatry, which makes it possible for two psychiatrists in good faith to come to entirely different conclusions.[9]

There is also evidence that psychiatrists with different theoretical orientations, and even from different countries, tend to view patients differently. Their personal values, social and political biases can also influence the content and perspective of a report. Changes in psychiatric policy, either by the American Psychiatric Association or by a group of psychiatrists can have a profound influence on how a person is labeled. There is also evidence that the personality of the psychiatrist conducting an interview or the setting in which it takes place can influence the material revealed by the patient. The unreliability and inaccuracy of psychiatric reports can affect the defendant both in general and in specific ways. If, for example, a psychiatrist perceives the defendant negatively it will affect the tone of the report. More specifically, the psychiatrist may make negative statements about the defendant, for example, by giving a poor prognosis for future behavior. Such a prognosis is read with much interest by the judge and may accordingly affect the sentence.

These limitations of the psychiatric method make the possibility of bias even more likely in psychiatric presentence reports than in probation reports. This possibility of bias is present despite the belief by the psychiatrists interviewed that they are functioning in the role of "friend of the court," and independent, impartial professionals. The possibility that the professional is likely to identify with the system with which he is associated is largely ignored by the courts.[10]

From the defendant's perspective this potential lack of impartiality is more damaging in the case of the psychiatric presentence report than the probationary presentence report because of the general role in which a psychiatrist is identified only with the interests of his patient, a role not usually shared by probation officers. Because the probation officer is not linked with the patient-therapist relationship, nor with the need to build rapport, in order to obtain more material in the interview, the defendant is less likely to have a misperception of the probation officer's role in the presentence investigation.

The possibility that a probation officer can make a mistake of fact and the possible detrimental effect of this has been used as an argument in favor of disclosure of the presentence report. Such a mistake of fact can also have a serious effect on the psychiatric report. In Philadelphia, for example, the court clinic usually waits for the probation report before writing the psychiatric report. This information is used by the psychiatrist in formulating his report, and thus any error made by the probation officer could influence the whole tenor of the psychiatric report in subtle and damaging ways.

Apart from the probation report, however, the psychiatrist does not use outside sources for the preparation of the report in the same way as does the probation officer. For this reason, one of the major arguments against disclosure of the probation report does not apply to psychiatric reports. The problem of sources drying up, the violation of trust of family members and other informants as well as outside agencies are some of the reasons given for nondisclosure of reports by those who oppose such disclosure, especially probation officers themselves.

The final argument which is particularly important for our purposes turns on the possible negative effect disclosure might have on the defendant himself. There are many references in the literature on probation presentence reports to exceptions being made for psychiatric data concerning the defendant, and many of those who are in favor of disclosure in general consider that an exception should be made in the case of psychological information. The assumption here is that disclosure of such information potentially can harm the defendant and hinder his chances for rehabilitation. If the defendant has access to a report, goes the argument, "that suddenly strips his personality naked, he will deny the picture as it is shown and reject the help that is accordingly offered."[11]

There is, however, no psychiatric research which provides data supporting this view. One could just as readily argue (as some have) that it is therapeutic for the defendant to know how he is seen by the psychiatrist and what areas the psychiatrist feels he should work on to change. He is also more likely to feel that he has been dealt with fairly and openly. There is also the view that the absence of disclosure may make him resentful and unamenable to therapy. Some psychiatrists consider that the defendant should know the contents of the report. One in fact, when interviewed, told of his practice of dictating the report in the presence of the defendant, "so he knows what is going in it." When the report is completed, the psychiatrist asks the defendant, "Can you think of anything good about yourself that I can add?" This is hardly a substitute for the right of rebuttal, but it does make the defendant aware of what is in the report and gives him some feeling of participation.

The potential harm caused by disclosure of psychiatric information may depend in part on how the report is written. There are psychiatrists (including the one quoted above) who believe that it is entirely possible to write a report which is harmless to the defendant but nevertheless as helpful to the court.

In view of the dearth of data supporting the allegation of potential harm to the defendant, the argument may be made that the defendant's rights outweigh the possibility of harm to him.

CONCLUSION

This paper has sought to examine the role of the psychiatrist in the preparation of presentence reports and the implications of that role. The peculiar nature of the psychiatrist-defendant relationship here has been seen as a perversion of the general patient-therapist relationship. The relative power of the psychiatrist and the defendant in the system has been discussed, with a power balance having been shown to have serious negative ramifications for the defendant.

The effect of the defendant's powerlessness vis-à-vis the psychiatrist in the evaluation process is multiplied by the defendant's inability to either know the contents of the psychiatric presentence report or to challenge the report. Comparisons were made between the probation presentence report and the psychiatric report to indicate to both that the defendant can, if anything, be more seriously harmed by nondisclosure of the psychiatric report than the probation report and also that disclosure potentially helps him less.

Because of the nature of psychiatric testimony, even knowing the contents of the report may not make it possible to rebut the information contained therein, as by contrast knowing the inaccurate information about one's arrest record in a probation report can readily lead to rebuttal. Thus the only effective process whereby the defendant could help himself to "rebut" the psychiatric view of him in the report would be in the preparation and production of a report by "his" psychiatrist.

The testimony of the court psychiatrist does not, as some believe, necessarily assist in clarifying issues, since the court psychiatrists are so locked into the system that their evidence is given great weight. As one psychiatrist put it: "We are not cross-examined too much, because of our reputation. They don't monkey with us." Cross-examination may assist in questioning some of the statements made in the report, but positive evidence would have to come from another psychiatric evaluation.

Thus, the defendant is locked into a system from which he cannot escape. The increased role of psychiatry in the legal process encourages more and more judges to use psychatric presentence reports in sentencing. The defendant has to be evaluated, both because he may not realize the adversary nature of the process and because a refusal to cooperate will negatively affect his position at sentencing. He may not be able to see what the psychiatrist has written about him and even if he does, he has little opportunity to alter any impression made on the judge by the contents of the report.

NOTES

1. For detailed descriptions of the several functions of psychiatric court clinics, see Harman (1969), Seligson (1956), and Russell (1969).

2 In my interviews, more judges said that the recommendation was the most important part of the report than any other part (Bohmer, 1973).

3. These statements come from informal interviews (1972-1976) conducted by the author at court psychiatric clinics in Philadelphia.

4. The results of these interviews are reported in Bohmer (1973 and 1975).

5. See Scott (1966).

6. For a full treatment of this subject see DeWitt (1958) and Slovenko (1966).

7. E.g., Oklahoma, where the defendant is advised by the court as to the factual contents and conclusions in the probation presentence report. Okla. Stat. Tit. 22 § 982 (1967). In Ohio, the probation officer testifies in open court and the defendant is given the right to examine him on his testimony. Ohio Rev. Code § 2947.06.

8. There is an extensive bibliography (but by no means all inclusive) of reports, reviews, articles, and cases in supporting disclosure of probation presentence reports in Buchea v. Sullivan (1972).

9. For one of the most comprehensive analysis of this and related issues, see Ziskin (1975).

10. E.g., "In upholding the validity of pre-sentence reports, the Supreme Court assumed that a probation department functions in an autonomous role, mediating impartially between the court and the defendant. In reality, this is not at all the case. . . . A probation department's independence and impartiality are inevitably tainted by its involvement with the organizational motives and designs of the court itself" (Blumberg, 1967).

11. Keve (1960). Note that Keve is a probation officer and not a psychiatrist.

REFERENCES

American Psychiatric Association (1973). "Principles of medical ethics with annotations especially applicable to psychiatry." American Journal of Psychiatry, 130(September):1057.

——— (1975). Confidentiality and third parties. Task Force Report (June).

BLUMBERG, A. (1967). Criminal justice. Chicago. Quadrangle.

BOHMER, C. (1973). "Judicial use of psychiatric reports in the sentencing of sex offenders." Journal of Psychiatry and Law, 1(summer):223, 235.

——— (1975). "Judicial use of psychiatric reports in the sentencing of sex offenders." Dissertation presented to the University of Pennsylvania (spring).

Buchea v. Sullivan (1972). 262 Ore. 222, 226-227, 497 P.2d 1169, 1171-1172.

DeWITT, C. (1958). Privileged communications between physician and patient. Springfield, Ill.: Charles C Thomas.

GREENWOOD, E. (1971). "Attributes of a profession." Pp. 3-16 in R.M. Pavalko (ed.), Social perspectives on occupations. Itasco, Ill.: Peacock.

HERMAN, F. (1969). "Social issues and the court psychiatric clinic." Federal Probation, 33(September):37.

HINCKS, M. (1944). "In opposition to rule 34(c)(2) proposed federal rules." Federal Probation, (October/December):7.

In re Lifschutz (1970). 2 Cal. 3d 415, 467 P.2d 557, 85 Cal. Rptr. 829.

KEVE, P. (1960). The Probation Officer Investigates, 10.

RUSSELL, D. (1969). "Massachusetts court clinics: A study of its administration and community aspects." International Journal of Offender Therapy, 13:140.

SCOTT, R. (1966). "Professionals and complex organizations." P. 226 in H.M. Vollmer and D.L. Mills (eds.), Professionalization. Englewood Cliffs, N.J.: Springfield, Ill.: Charles C Thomas.

SELIGSON, S. (1956). "The psychiatric court clinic." Temple Law Quarterly, 29:347.

SLOVENKO, R. (1966). Psychotherapy, confidentiality, and privileged communication. Springfield, Ill.: Charles C Thomas.

SZASZ, T. (1965). Psychiatric justice. New York: Macmillan.

ZISKIN, J. (1975). Coping with psychiatric and psychological testimony. Beverly Hills, Calif.: Law and Psychology Press.

DUANE C. McBRIDE
SUSAN G. DALTON
Miami School of Medicine

7

CRIMINAL JUSTICE DIVERSION FOR WHOM?

The American criminal justice system was developed within the context of Enlightenment concepts and the religious philosophy of the Quakers. It was during this historical period that philosophers and scientists began the application of rationalist assumptions to the control of human behavior (see Carter et al., 1975). The classical criminologists assumed that man was rational and hedonistic (pleasure seeking and pain avoiding). Within this framework, it was argued that human beings would not violate the law if doing so caused them pain. It was further argued that the severity of the punishment should fit the crime; that is the severity of the punishment should be greater for those crimes which society decreed to be the most serious (for a discussion of the criminological thought of the rationalists, see Phillipson, 1923).

While this rationalist view of punishment came to dominate penal philosophy, the particular type of punishment that came to be used in the United States was developed by the Quakers in Pennsylvania in the latter part of the nineteenth century (see Barnes, 1969:83-150).

AUTHORS' NOTE: The authors wish to thank James Ward, Larry Bennett, David Pickens, and Barbara Radin of the Miami TASC Project for their cooperation in collecting the data necessary for this report.

According to Quaker thought, punishment should take the form of confinement in which a law violator would have the time to reflect on his wrongdoing, see the error of his ways, and thereupon change his behavior. In the development of the criminal justice and penal systems in the United States, the assumptions of the rationalists and the Quakers were integrated. Punishment took the form of confinement in the penitentiary and varied in length by the assumed severity of the crime committed.

This system of criminal justice and penal philosophy has been dominant in the United States for the last 200 years. While modifications have occurred within the system, as recent literature has indicated (Quinney, 1974; Zimring and Hawkins, 1973), the system is primarily oriented toward the confinement of criminal offenders for purposes of punishment and for the protection of society. It is the purpose of this paper to examine briefly the development of alternatives to incarceration, discuss the types of offenses for which alternatives to incarceration are used, and to present data on the characteristics of those who accept diversion compared to the characteristics of those in the target population who did not accept diversion.

THE DEVELOPMENT OF ALTERNATIVES

In recent years, there has been an attempt to change the basic application of criminal justice by critically reviewing the scope of its application and by using alternatives to incarceration based on different assumptions about the causes of crime. Those who have attempted to develop modern, systematic alternatives to the traditional criminal justice system have generally focused their efforts on two types of programs: (1) those that decriminalize or at least deformalize particular types of offenses, and (2) those that attempt to deal more directly and effectively with the assumed causes of criminal behavior.

The first type of program attempts to remove particular types of behavior from the jurisdiction of the criminal law.

Such a program has a great potential for removing a large proportion of cases from the criminal justice system. Any examination of the cases processed by the court system shows that the majority of those cases are minor and include such offenses as drunkenness, disorderly conduct, possession of marijuana, loitering, minor property disputes, some moral charges, and familial disputes. Efforts to remove these offenses from the court system have taken two directions. Legislatures have begun to decriminalize certain offenses, specifically those involving the use of alcohol and, to a lesser extent, marijuana use. Many jurisdictions have also attempted to develop a system for the informal handling of minor offenses (e.g., see Palmer, 1975). Within such a system, law students or other professionals serve as arbitrators in minor disputes without the imposition (or legal protection) of the court.

The second type of alternative assumes the validity of the law but attempts to stop or reduce criminal behavior by means other than incarceration. Throughout most of this century, researchers, clinicians, and practitioners in the criminal justice field have noted the inequality and ineffectiveness of the traditional system. However, there has been considerable public resistance to any attempt to modify or modernize the penal system. Ideas of punishment and doing penance have proved exceedingly durable.

In the 1960s under the Johnson administration, there was a major focus on crime and delinquency (President's Commission, 1967). A task force was formed to prepare a broad report on the subject. If found that the traditional penal system was not successful in dealing with crime, that rates of recidivism were high, and that penal systems were primarily operating as socializing institutions to further criminal behavior. The task force concluded that if crime was to be reduced, alternatives to incarceration had to be developed.

Two major traditions in criminological thought have had a major impact in the development of alternatives to incarceration, differential association, and, especially, labeling theory. In 1950, Clemmer noted that jails and prisons function as learning environments in which individuals learn roles and behavior that enable them to function in a penal institution. The behavior and attitudes learned included socialization into criminal and other roles that are not particularly useful in an outside environment. Because imprisonment socializes incarcerated individuals into roles that could only be played in prison, Clemmer (1950) argued that the prison experience itself was responsible for high recidivism rates.

The works of criminologists such as Lemert (1973, 1976) and Becker (1973) have had a major impact on the development of alternatives to imprisonment. Within the labeling perspective, most individuals are seen as engaging at one time or another in law-violating behavior. It is also assumed that certain individuals, because of society's functional needs (Erikson, 1962, 1966), are processed through the criminal justice system and incarcerated. As a result of that processing and labeling, the individual, via a symbolic interaction process, adopts a criminal self-concept and organizes his behavior around that self-concept. By the apprehension, processing, and public labeling, what may have been sporadic, episodic behavior becomes the core aspect of self and the cause of continuous criminal behavior.

WHO SHOULD BE DIVERTED?

Today diversion programs exist in almost every state. Over 120 programs are currently in operation around the country (American Bar Association, 1975). In the development of proposals to establish diversion programs, one of the major questions addressed is that of defining the type of offender for whom diversion is a viable alternative. Unfortunately, the answer to that question often becomes a political issue, basing diversion criteria on public opinion rather than research or careful analysis. Diversion programs have been a part of juvenile justice systems for many years. Today, however, there are diversion programs available for almost any type of adult offender except for those displaying extreme violence.

Status Offenders. As a category, juvenile status offenders, (e.g., truants, runaways) have been the major focus and justification for diversion programs. It is for this category that the rationale and logic of diversion has appeared to be the most compelling. The traditional criminal justice and penal systems are based on the assumption that crime is a rational act and involves a weighing of reward and cost which can be prevented if the cost is made sufficiently high.

Many criminologists view the problem as being the legal system which defines the use of particular drugs, for example, as illegal, resulting in the unavailability of the drugs which leads to an almost inevitable relationship between crime and drugs (Schur, 1969). For the addict, drugs are expensive but have to be obtained. Frequently, the only means of obtaining the necessary funds to purchase drugs is to engage in illegal, income-producing behavior. Many studies have found an extensive relationship between the use of illicit drugs and crime. A large proportion of those arrested has been found to be regular users of illicit drugs (Eckerman et al., 1971; Ford et al., 1975; McBride, 1977), and an equally large proportion of drug users in treatment has been found to have regularly engaged in criminal behavior (Greenberg and Adler, 1974).

Criminologists and clinicians for years have argued that the criminal behavior of addicts is at least partially based on the fact of their addiction (O'Donnell, 1969). Thus, the logic has been that the only viable way to reduce the criminal behavior of drug users is to treat and hopefully stop their addiction. Diversion from the criminal justice system has existed for drug users in the form of civil commitment in some states for 25 years and on the federal level for the last decade (see Petersen, 1974). Currently such diversion programs for drug users are administratively under the auspices of the Department of Justice.

The Department of Justice's Law Enforcement Assistance Administration (LEAA) has initiated and funded a number of large scale projects entitled Treatment Alternatives to Street Crime (TASC). These TASC programs serve as a liaison between criminal justice and community treatment structures. Essentially, TASC programs were to divert drug-using arrestees (only those charged with violence were not acceptable) into ongoing, existing, drug treatment programs. The original charge is held in abeyance until treatment is completed. As is the case with all types of diversion programs (and social programs in general) evaluation is difficult, but TASC programs have shown a definite need for their services (McBride and Bennett, forthcoming). They have been able to recruit clients and perform the difficult task of convincing the police and the courts to cooperate.

Misdemeanors and Minor Felonies. While most media and public attention is focused on the major crimes involving major property loss, or severe personal injury, most cases in the criminal justice system involve what are essentially minor acts: disturbing the peace, loitering, drunkenness, disorderly conduct, and minor property disputes. Most of the existing diversion programs focus on serving this type of minor offense (American Bar Association, 1975). These programs attempt to work out mutual agreements between parties in conflict (Palmer, 1975), to encourage accused individuals to participate in a restitution program, or to encourage participation in structured treatment programs providing counseling and minimal supervision. These last two approaches have been used extensively with juvenile offenders.

Felonies. While most programs focus on removing juveniles, minor offenders, and status offenders from the criminal justice system, other programs have shown that adult offenders charged with major felonies are viable candidates for diversion. For example, as Lamb and

Goertzel (1975) reported in *Federal Probation*, Ellsworth House in San Mateo County, California was designed to provide diversion facilities for adults whose offenses included armed robbery, burglary, grand theft, receiving stolen property, assault with a deadly weapon, various drug offenses, forgery, auto theft, and voluntary and involuntary manslaughter. Ellsworth House is a residential therapeutic community with an emphasis on group therapy, counseling, and such auxiliary services as job and educational counseling and job placement. The existence and success of such a facility suggest we can assume diversion to be a viable alternative for most types of offenses.

Initially, most diversion programs focused on first offenders, juveniles, and young adults. It was assumed that this group, as labeling theory implies, should be diverted from the labeling and incarceration process in order to avoid becoming a secondary deviant. However, as a report by the American Bar Association (1975) indicates, many programs in the last few years have provided services to those considered to be the older and habitual offenders. The continuing acceptance of these programs suggests that there are very few limitations as to who should be diverted.

As has been discussed, one way of assessing the feasibility and utilitiy of social programs, such as criminal justice diversion, is to examine the populations for whom they can be applied. To a brief extent that has been done, but evaluation of offender types is extremely complex and difficult (Klein, 1976). Most programs have not existed for a sufficient length of time to properly evaluate them. Additionally, research based on methodologically sound design does not exist that would enable concluding statements about the effectiveness of diversion (see Gibbons and Blake, 1976). At this time what can be said is that most diversion programs have been able to recruit and provide services to clients in sufficient numbers so as to at least imply a need for their existence.

As with most social programs, criminal justice diversion programs are most frequently examined, assessed, and discussed in terms of their target populations. Much is usually written about who the appropriate target populations are for specific programs and whether or not those programs reach their target populations. However, examination of whom within the target population the social program selects, attracts, or provides for, is generally neglected. Considerable thought, research, and politics go into decisions about who should be diverted. But perhaps equally important are the characteristics of those in the target population not served. Such differences may have major implications for a program's underlying philosophy and ability to reach its goals.

In an attempt to compare target population and client characteristics, data were collected from June through August 1974 on all individuals arrested and processed through the Metropolitan Dade County Jail, in cooperation witih the Dade County, Florida TASC Program. The data were collected by TASC interviewers as part of their program for recruiting clients. Information was collected on demographic characteristics, income, education, occupation, and drug use patterns. For purposes of analysis the respondents were divided into three groups: (1) diverted arrestees (these individuals who currently used illicit drugs, volunteered for the program and with the court's approval were diverted); (2) other arrested drug users (these individuals who were eligible for diversion in that they met the criteria developed by the TASC program but they chose to take their chances with the criminal justice system); and (3) the remainder of the arrested population (those who did not currently use illicit drugs and therefore did not meet the basic eligibility criteria for this particular diversion program. A few individuals (37) who were eligible for diversion and who sought to participate in the TASC program but whom the court would not divert were eliminated from the analysis.

FINDINGS

Demographic Characteristics and Diversion

The data presented in Table 1 show that those in the arrested population currently using illicit drugs are generally more likely to be male, black, and under 25.

The data also show some major differences between eligible individuals and those actually diverted. Those diverted from the criminal justice system are slightly more likely to be male (79.1% versus 77.9%) and significantly

Table 1. Demographic Characteristics of Diverted Arrestees Compared to Other Drug Users and Remainder of Arrested Population in Metropolitan Dade County, Florida, Jail (in percentages)

Characteristics	Diverted Arrestees N = 148	Other Drug Users N = 1,901	Remainder of Arrested Population N = 1,629	Total N = 3,673*
Sex				
Male	79.1	77.9	73.4	76.0
Female	20.9	22.1	26.6	24.0

x^2 = 10.4, df = 2, significant at better than .01 level.
V = .053
*Information was missing on 16 individuals.

Ethnic Group	N = 149	N = 1,907	N = 1,637	N = 3,693*
White	19.5	35.0	30.5	32.4
Black	73.8	58.5	40.5	51.1
Spanish	6.7	5.8	28.3	15.8
Other	0.0	0.7	0.7	0.6

x^2 = 254.7, df = 6, significant at better than .001 level.
V = .053
*Information was missing on 1 individual.

Age	N = 149	N = 1,902	N = 1,631	N = 3,682*
Under 17	0.0	0.1	0.1	0.1
17-25	70.5	73.8	47.0	61.8
26-34	26.8	21.3	25.6	23.4
Over 35	2.7	4.7	27.3	14.7

x^2 = 433.3, df = 6, significant at better than .001 level.
V = .243
*Information was missing on 12 individuals.

more likely to be black (73.8% versus 58.5%). Within the eligible target population, TASC ended up diverting into community treatment clients who were more likely to be black and male.

Table 2. Net Weekly Income, Educational Attainment, and Usual Occupational Status of Diverted Arrestees Compared to Other Drug Users and Remainder of Arrested Population, Metropolitan Dade County, Florida, Jail (in percentages)

	Diverted Arrestees N = 148	Other Drug Users N = 1,906	Remainder of Arrested Population N = 1,636	Total N = 3,690*
Net Weekly Income				
None	54.1	49.0	35.2	43.1
Under $75	10.8	8.0	8.6	8.4
$75-$100	15.5	15.2	16.4	15.7
$101-$150	13.5	16.2	20.4	17.9
Over $150	6.1	11.6	19.4	14.9
x^2 = 99.1, df = 8, significant at better than .001 level.				
V = .116				
*Information was missing on 4 individuals.				
Educational Attainment	N = 149	N = 1,903	N = 1,628	N = 3,680*
0-8 years	6.0	6.1	16.1	10.5
9-11 years	52.3	45.8	36.1	41.8
12 years	30.2	36.7	34.4	35.4
13-15 years	10.7	9.8	9.3	9.6
16 years and over	0.7	1.7	4.1	2.7
x^2 = 134.6, df = 8, significant at better than .001 level.				
V = .135				
*Information was missing on 14 individuals.				
Usual Occupational Status	N = 144	N = 1,756	N = 1,535	N = 3,435*
Professional, technical, and administrative	0.7	2.3	5.7	3.7
Sales, clerical, skilled, and semi-skilled	8.3	17.9	22.4	19.5
Laborers and service workers	36.8	32.9	39.2	35.9
Not employed	54.2	46.9	32.7	40.9
x^2 = 102.2, df = 6, significant at better than .001 level.				
V = .122				
*Information was missing on 259 individuals.				

Socioeconomic Status and Diversion

As most research on arrested or incarcerated populations has shown, the criminal justice system in this country primarily deals with a population of lower class individuals. However, there is some variance in the social class characteristics of those arrested. In Table 2, data are presented regarding differences in income, education, and occupation between diverted and other drug users.

Income and Diversion. As the data presented in Table 2 indicate, most of those arrested have very little legitimate income. Illicit drug users are more likely to have no legitimate income than those who did not use illicit drugs. Drug users who are diverted are more likely to have no legitimate income (54.1%) than other drug users (49%). Similar differences are apparent at the other extreme of the income categories. Of those diverted, only 6.1% have legitimate incomes of over $150 per week compared to 11.6% of the other drug users.

The data suggest that those who end up being diverted are a lower income group even within a population of low income individuals. Those drug users with higher legitimate incomes chose not to participate in an alternative to the criminal justice system. Rather, they chose to take their chances within the system.

Education and Diversion. The data presented in Table 2 show that those arrested have little formal education. Overall, the majority of individuals (52.3%) had not finished high school and only 2.7% had graduated from college.

The data also show that drug users in general are less likely to have had as many years of education as non-drug users. This might possibly be due to age differences. As the data in Table 1 indicate, illicit drug users are much more likely to be ages 17-25 than nonusers. Thus, some could be too young to have finished much education, but most of them are old enough to have at least finished high school. Diverted arrestees are more likely not to have finished high school (58.3%) than nondiverted drug users (51.9%). This difference is probably not due to age because there were more 17-25 year olds (73.8%) among the nondiverted drug users than among those diverted (70.5%).

Occupation and Diversion. Arrestees who use illicit drugs are more likely to hold lower status jobs or to be unemployed. As was the case with education, this could be a reflection of age differences. Generally, unemployment rates are higher for younger age groups. However, the data also show that diverted arrestees who are generally a little older than those drug users not diverted are less likely to hold jobs in the highest status category (0.7% versus 2.3%). Diverted arrestees are more likely to hold laboring or service jobs (36.8%) than nondiverted drug users (32.9%) and to be unemployed (54.2% compared to 46.9% of the nondiverted drug users).

All of the social class indicators are consistent. Those arrested are generally from lower class populations. Among this basically lower class population, drug users are even more likely to be lower class. Among illicit drug users, diverted drug users are more likely to be lower class than nondiverted drug users.

The data presented in these two tables indicate that of those eligible for diversion (the target population), those most likely to accept the diversion program are blacks, males, low income individuals, high school dropouts, and unemployed. Whites, at least those who finished high school and those who were employed, were more likely to take their chances with the criminal justice system.

A number of things are implied by the data. First of all, it should probably be noted that the Dade County TASC diversion project cannot be accused of racial or economic discrimination. Essentially, those individuals who accepted a diversion program were those individuals who historically are most likely not to fare well in the traditional criminal justice system. Those accepting diversion are those who criminologists have frequently found are more likely to be convicted and receive harsher sentences. In that sense, a diversion program such as TASC offers an important alternative to this population.

However, the characteristics of the population willing to accept diversion have some implications for the success of the diversion program and the types of services the program needs to offer. It certainly can be argued that the TASC program attracted a population in need of its services. TASC diverted these individuals into community treatment programs which offered them, in addition to the traditional therapeutic services, auxiliary services such as vocational counseling and placement and educational tutoring. But the population diverted also caused severe problems for the survival of TASC. The TASC diverted clients generally had higher split rates, more drug use, and more rearrests than other clients in the treatment program. TASC had diverted a population very much in need of services, but also one that requried the most services and was more likely not to succeed in treatment.

Diversion programs should be aware not only of their target population but whom within that target population they are serving. Such information could be important in planning or modifying services designed for the whole target population and in providing essential data that must be considered in any evaluation of the programs.

REFERENCES

American Bar Association Commission on Correctional Facilities Services (1975). "Pre-trial criminal justice intervention technique and action programs." Washington, DC: American Bar Association.

BARNES, H. (1969). The repression of crime. Montclair, NJ: Patterson Smith.

BECKER, H. (1973). "Labeling theory reconsidered." Pp. 117-208 in H.S. Becker (ed.), Outsiders. New York: Free Press.

CARTER, R., McGEE, R., and NELSON, E. (1975). Corrections in America. Philadelphia: J.B. Lippincott.

CLEMMER, D. (1950). "On imprisonment as a source of criminality." Journal of Criminal Law, Criminology and Police Science, 41(September):311-319.

ECKERMAN, W., BATES, J., RACHAL, J. and POOLE, W. (1971). "Drug use and arrest charges (NTIS #PB 251965)." Drug Enforcement Administration. Washington DC: U.S. Government Printing Office.

ERIKSON, K. (1962). "Notes on the sociology of deviance." Social Problems, 9(spring):307-314.

——— (1966). Wayward Puritans. New York: John Wiley.

FORD, A., HAUSER, H., and JACKSON, E., Jr. (1975). "Use of drugs among persons admitted to a county jail." Public Health Reports, 90:504-508.

GIBBONS, D. and BLAKE, G. (1976). "Evaluating the impact of juvenile diversion programs." Crime and Delinquency, (October):411-420.

GREENBERG, S. and ADLER, F. (1974). "Crime and addiction: An empirical analysis of the literature, 1920-1973." Contemporary Drug Problems, (summer): 221-270.

KLEIN, M. (1976). "Issues and realities in police diversion programs." Crime and Delinquency, (October):421-427.

LAMB, H. and GOERTZEL, V. (1975). "A community alternative to county jail: The hopes and realities." Federal Probation, 39(March):33-39.

LEMERT, E. (1973). Human deviance, social problems, and social control. Englewood Cliffs, NJ: Prentice-Hall.

——— (1976). "Instead of court: Diversion in juvenile justice." In R.M. Carter and M.W. Klein (eds.), Back on the street. Englewood Cliffs, NJ: Prentice-Hall.

McBRIDE, D. (1977). "The relationship between the type of drug use and arrest charge in an arrested population." National Institute on Drug Abuse Research Monograph, Drug Use and Crime. Washington, DC: U.S. Government Printing Office.

——— and BENNETT, A. (forthcoming). "The impact of criminal justice diversion on an existing community treatment structure." Drug Forum, 8(1).

O'DONNELL, J. (1969). Narcotic addicts in Kentucky. Washington, DC: U.S. Government Printing Office.

PALMER, J. (1975). "Pre-arrest diversion: The night prosecutor's program in Columbus, Ohio." Crime and Delinquency, 21(April):100-108.

PETERSEN, D. (1974). "Some reflections on compulsory treatment of addiction." Pp. 143-169 in J.A. Inciardi and C.D. Chambers (eds.), Drugs and the criminal justice system. Beverly Hills, Calif.: Sage.

PHILLIPSON, C. (1923). Three criminal law reformers: Becarria, Benthan, Romilly. London: Denter.

President's Commission on Law Enforcement and Administration of Justice (1967). Task Force Report: Juvenile delinquency and youth crime. Washington, DC: U.S. Government Printing Office.

QUINNEY, R. (ed., 1974). Criminal justice in America. Boston: Little, Brown.

SCHUR, E. (1969). Our criminal society. Englewood Cliffs, N.J.: Prentice-Hall.

SMITH, R. (1973). "Diversion: New label—Old practices." Pp. 39-56 in New approaches to diversion and treatment of juvenile offenders. U.S. Department of Justice. Washington, DC: U.S. Government Printing Office.

ZIMRING, F. and HAWKINS, G. (1973). Deterrence: The legal threat in crime control. Chicago: University of Chicago Press.

Arnold Binder
University of California, Irvine

8

DIVERSION AND THE JUSTICE SYSTEM: Evaluating the Results

The scientific method was developed over the years to provide some degree of control over the errors and biases that enter into human decision-making. It specifies a certain orderliness and precision in the way data are collected, analyzed, and interpreted in the realm of inquiry encompassed by science.

Similar errors and biases enter into all areas of human decision-making, and efforts are made to reduce them to tolerable levels by the various means available. In particular, over approximately the last generation, considerable attention has been directed toward developing systematic methods for evaluating social programs. The developing process has been strongly influenced by the scienfific method, due in no small part to the fact that most of the evaluators have backgrounds in the social and behavioral sciences.

To illustrate the relationship, consider the broad specification of the scientific method as: (1) formulate hypotheses or select among hypotheses previously formulated, (2) deduce consequences from the hypotheses and develop measures or indicators, (3) collect relevant data, and (4) relate outcome data to indicators of consequences to establish credibility of hypotheses. If you substitute the word "goals" for the word "hypotheses" in the above specification and adjust for the condition that goals are or are not achieved rather than confirmed in an inferential chain, the scientific method becomes precisely the evaluation method presented in recent textbooks on evaluation (see, for example, Weiss, 1972).

I do realize that the horizons of evaluation have expanded from that basic format, but I believe that ancestry is still very much in evidence. For example, it seems that "Goal Free Evaluation" has largely substituted the formal evaluator for project staff in the decision-making process. The goal free evaluator enters the domain in which a service is being offered, does a needs assessment in the area of interest, sets up procedures to determine what is being accomplished, and compares needs and accomplishments. The process is the same but the point of departure is further down the pike.

Now, if there is any arena in which the evaluation enterprise is superactive, it is in diversion. There are many reasons for the state of affairs, but high on any list must be the fact that diversion has been rolling along rapidly and widely in recent years, and the rolling has been possible only because of federal oiling, which of course requires evaluation.

There have been so many evaluations, in fact, that in recent years we have been seeing many evaluations of evaluations. But, despite that superactivity and evaluations of evaluations over a period of perhaps 10 years, there are not many definite statements that can be made about the evaluative results of diversion.

Here are few examples from the area of juvenile diversion that illustrate how far we are from definite knowledge. Dixon and Wright (1975:81) reviewed the evaluative literature on juvenile diversion under an NSF grant and concluded "some methods of delinquency prevention or reduction are more effective than others. Educational and vocational projects, community treatment programs, the use of volunteers and nonprofessionals, and youth service bureaus all show some sign of effectiveness." Now that is not a ringing endorsement, but contrast it with the positions of various other evaluators. Although, Lundman et al (1976:307) included more than diversion in their survey of the delinquency prevention literature, their coverage within diversion was much like that of Dixon and Wright. However, they concluded, *"it appears unlikely that any of these projects prevented delinquent behavior."* And after a review directed at diversion more narrowly, Higgins (1975:5) concluded, "This review has reached an inescapable conclusion. While the early minor offender deserves the attention of policy makers, no current prevention strategies can be confidently recommended. The best evidence to date indicates that a major tactic of prevention projects, diverting youth from the criminal justice system, does not reduce delinquency."

As an example of the same level of confusion in the realm of adult diversion, we have the disparate viewpoints of Fishman (1975) and Zimring (1975). Fishman evaluated rehabilitation and diversion programs in New York City (including juvenile as well as adult services), and concluded that diversion was a resounding failure in reducing recidivism and actually contributed to overall increased crime. Zimring (1975:1) evaluated Fishman's evaluation and reported, "the data generated by the study do not, in my view, support the inferences drawn in the final report." He took specific exception to the claims that the programs failed to reduce rearrests and added to an increase in crime.

There are many reasons for the divergence in opinion regarding the effectiveness of diversion. Uppermost, perhaps, is the fact that the outcome data are far from crystal clear. But I believe that is far from the full story; indeed my goal is to dwell upon three other reasons that have not received the attention I believe they deserve.

The first of these stems from a question of definition. In a recent book on diversion, for which he was coeditor, Klein (1976a:74) provides the following definition, "We shall mean by *diversion* any process employed by components of the criminal justice system (police, prosecution, courts, corrections) to turn suspects and/or offenders away from the formal system or to a 'lower' level in the system."

If that is one's definition, then there are clearly certain evaluative questions that are inappropriate. For example, one does not evaluate whether or not diversion as a process is effective for juveniles. Let me emphasize that Klein's definition encompasses each of the following under diversion: police discretion, counsel and release, informal probation, and home supervision, and thereby makes diversion an inseparable part of the juvenile justice system. It is abundantly clear that the juvenile justice system could not operate without diversion so defined; indeed, the key element in juvenile court law is diversion as stated in some such form as preference for the "least restrictive alternative" or "return to the family," in terms of the "best interests of the child." Imagine, if you will, the state of affairs without diversion in that broad sense whereby every curfew violator, every runaway or truant, every child reported by a parent as ungovernable is subjected to full justice processing, including court hearings and possibly treatment if the petition is sustained.

In a later part of the book containing that definition, Klein (1976b:313) discusses certain evaluative data dealing with police diversion in Los Angeles County. He concludes, "we have learned that the diversion process is at best minimal. The police are not currently connecting many juvenile offenders with resources in the community."

The definition has clearly changed—now diversion necessarily encompasses referral to a community agency. And in several related papers, the same writer (Klein and Teilmann, 1976; Teilmann, Klein, and Styles, 1975) has argued that police diversion is not really diversion because it is used as a substitute for counsel and release rather than for petitioning. In this case diversion seems to require an intent followed by a revocation of intent.

Finally, a strange condensation of all those perspectives is encompassed in a very recent paper by Klein (1976c: 427). He defines diversion in the broadest sense (Klein, 1976a:74) to include counsel and release, varies the meaning in numerous ways over the course of writing, and concludes that diversion is doomed. In the words of the paper, "*Diversion has been appended rather than incorporated.* Among the police, we predict for it a short, inconclusive life." One must read this logical zig-zag to believe it.

As another example of confusion of definition, we have the paper of Lundman (1976) in which he differentiated "diversion programs" from the traditional forms of diversion (like counsel and release) by stating that diversion programs involve formal screening procedures, awareness of the possibilities of stigmatization, and availability of resources for referral. Yet, after evaluating the literature, he offers the following conclusion:

> Diversion programs are being implemented in the absence of adequate study of the effects of past practices. As noted, diversion is an old practice. Police officers have regularly warned and released more juveniles than they have arrested, while probation officers have routinely placed juveniles on informal probation as an alternative to the filing of a petition for a formal hearing. Despite this informal diversion, the juvenile crime rate has continued to increase. Thus one can at least question the adequacy of the assertion that formal diversion results in a decrease in juvenile recidivism. [1976:435]

In this case, the critical features of the definition are washed away in the process of a head spinning inferential leap.

The term diversion is precise enough to specify the bounds of a paper like this one—people within the criminal justice field read the title and are reasonably confident they know the broad bounds of discussion. But in terms of the specifics critical for program evaluation, consider some of the activities encompassed under the diversion rubric: court ordered counseling; community treatment programs; probation counseling in lieu of petitioning; probation referral to community agencies specializing in recreation, vocational and educational counseling, crisis intervention, family counseling, and individual psychotherapy; district attorney referral to community agencies of the various sorts; police probation; special police officers trained in the behavioral sciences; in-house, non-police counseling staff within police departments; and referral by police to community agencies of every conceivable sort. And the methods used with offenders include operant conditioning, as Transactional Analysis, Transcendental Meditation, Reality Therapy, Assertion Training, Moral Development, Systematic Desensitization, and so on.

When one concludes that diversion does not work, one may mean that referring youngsters to a facility containing handball courts does not change their delinquent behavior. I think the accumulating evidence from Patterson et al. (1968), Alexander and Parsons (1973), and Ku and Blew (1977) indicates that certain behavioral change approaches do indeed change behavior, including behavior that is technically defined as delinquent or criminal. I think it is equally evident that recreation progams, social case work, intensive psychotherapy, and counsel and release do not, in general, change delinquent or criminal behavior.

My position is similar to that of Klapmuts (1974:113) who stated,

> Currently, diversion from the criminal justice system has many different meanings, largely because the term does not accurately describe the different activities to which it is applied. The task of developing definitions and setting standards for the operation of diversion alternatives might be greatly simplified if the popularized notion of "diversion from the justice system" were discarded and replaced by terms descriptive of the various alternatives that may be invoked at each stage of traditional processing.

The recent report by Rutherford and McDermott (1976) as part of the National Evaluation Program stresses a similar point and presents a diversion typology based upon proximity of a program to justice system operations.

My second difficulty with diversion evaluation is the tendency to embellish the diversion process with excess conceptual baggage and then attack diversion because of faulty conceptualization. While Lundman (1976) has gone perhaps further than most in incorporating a labeling component in his very definition of a diversion program, many writers have justified diversion approaches on the basis of a labeling perspective. Indeed, the report that motivated the present diversionary thrust—The President's Commission on Law Enforcement and Administration of Justice (1967)—claimed the avoidance of stigmatization as one of the prime bases of diversion. Others who have taken the position include Lemert (1971), Cressey and McDermott (1973), Gemignani (1972), and Smith (1973).

There are two points I would like to make in this area. First, justification for diversion in terms of a theoretical structure that is no more empirically grounded than diversion itself is a precarious undertaking. Second, unless one justifies diversion solely on the basis of the avoidance of labeling, one cannot use arguments against labeling theory as arguments against diversion. If you think that the straw man is of my creation rather than someone else's, I urge you to read Lundman's (1976) article where he states that the results of labeling research question the adequacy of the argument that diversion decreases recidivism. In his terms, "This research [that is, labeling research] suggests that programs which rely on diversion to reduce recidivism are not likely to be any more successful than other types of programs" (1976:435-436).

I recognize that some advocates of the labeling position carry the labeling notion to such extremes that they seem to believe that if a youngster sees the words "I" and "criminal" on the same page, he will immediately adopt self-perceptions of hopeless criminality. But I am restricting my argument to those like Lemert (1972) and Kitsuse (1962) who require serious processing by the justice system and by the individual to expect the impact of labeling.

And biases such as these on the part of evaluators form the basis of the third of the difficulties I see in the area. These biases are determined by a large array of factors, but among them, it is clear that the constituency of the evaluator stands out prominently. By constituency I mean the sources of such goodies as income, promotion, prestige, status, and power. We are all as suspicious of the evaluator who also happens to be the designer of the project and its principal investigator, as we are of the evaluators who get substantial fees as members of a corporate team or as private consultants, with future fees dependent upon present performance. But, except when our research is directly attacked, we hardly ever seem suspicious of the academic evaluator whose coin of the realm is being critical. And particularly when creativity is lacking, being critical can carry one a long way in academic cricles.

Adams (1976) in his recent debate with Martinson (1976) provided an excellent example of the role of constituency in determining evaluative position. Adams pointed out that Martinson was more emphatic and certain in his condemnation of prison rehabilitation while appearing on the "60 Minutes" CBS broadcast than he was in his article in *Public Interest*.

Distortions resulting from the biases and expectancies of the investigator are common in the world of science as in the more mundane aspects of human endeavor. For example, in his famous book on scientific investigation, Beveridge (1961:144) states, "In nearly all matters the human mind has a strong tendency to judge in the light of its own experience, knowledge and prejudices rather than on the evidence presented."

And after discussing the treatment that the work of such people as Harvey, Pasteur, Semmelweis, Rontgen,

Mendel, and Waterston received at the hands of their colleagues, he states,

> It has been said that the reception of an original contribution to knowledge may be divided into three phases: during the first it is ridiculed as not true, impossible or useless; during the second, people say there may be something in it but it would never be of any practical use; and in the third and final phase, when the discovey has received general recognition, there are usually people who say that it is not original and has been anticipated by others. [1961:151-152]

I distinctly do not want to put diversion research in the same realm as the discovery of blood circulation or the discovery of X-rays or the formulation of the molecular theory of gases. My goal is the simpler one of showing that humans will be humans.

Consider the generally antidiversion paper by Higgins (1975). He places the review of Dixon and Wright (1975) in the category of evidence against the usefulness of diversion, and states about that work, "Also a recent review of about 100 delinquency prevention programs appearing in the literature since 1965 concluded, 'Indeed, no (prevention) method has been demonstrated to be consistently effective' " (1975:4). In fact, the general thrust of the Dixon and Wright survey is upon the differential effectiveness of various types of intervention rather than their uselessness. And their prime recommendation is, "The general trend to divert youth from the criminal justice system should be continued" (1975:63).

And here is another example—one for which I have particular sensitivity. Gibbons and Blake (1976) have recently published a paper that was originally presented at the meetings of the Pacific Sociological Association. Their bias becomes obvious in the first line of the paper: "One of the major current fads in criminal and juvenile justice programming is diversion of offenders from the justice systems" (1976:411). You can count on it, when diversion is referred to as a "fad," it will get harsh treatment. "Fad" is to the skeptical opposition what "exciting innovation" is to the advocate.

I quote from the Gibbons and Blake article:

> The Pre-Trial Intervention and Diversion Project, conducted in Huntington Beach and Costa Mesa, Calif., was intended to improve parent-child communication and coping skills. A control group of 34 youths and a treatment group numbering 130 youngsters were established by randomization. The follow-up period was six months. The findings from this study are severely limited: the follow-up period was too short for adequate assessment of impact, and the evaluation report fails to indicate the nature of the handling accorded to the control cases; and follow-up measures were restricted to re-arrest data, with no indication of other effects produced by the project. [1976:415]

Let us turn to the document (Binder, 1974) to which that severe criticism was directed. We find, first, that it is not the full evaluation report of the project as the above quote seems to imply, but the first annual report. How, then, could there be more than a six months follow-up since the very earliest cases had been seen only 11 months earlier, and a substantial case backlog had barely been built up for the six months evaluation? Further, let us consider the statement that the "evaluation report fails to indicate the nature of the handling accorded to the control cases." Sounds like irresponsible evaluating, does it not? But let us turn back to the evaluation (Binder, 1974). Here is what it says about the control group: "While no service is rendered by our staff to those in the control group, the police officers are, of course, free to provide whatever whatever service or referral they would have provided to these juveniles were the Youth Service Program not available" (p.11 of Appendix B). The comparison, for purposes of the evaluation, was between outcome data from normal police operations without the availability of Program counselors and from police operations plus diversion personnel. Seems like a sound design to me, as well as to the staff of the National Evaluation Program (Rutherford and McDermott, 1976:39) who argue, "Existing research . . . has not demonstrated that doing something (treatment, services) is necessarily better than not doing anything. . . . There is a crucial need to develop a research design that adequately compares doing 'something' with doing 'nothing'."

That covers two of their three points. Now about the third stating that "follow-up measures were restricted to re-arrest data." In fact, survey information was obtained from parents, youngsters, and police on a follow-up basis, and this information is discussed at some length in the report. One unique aspect in the approach was the use of a double-blind procedure where a telephone interviewer was indentified with a police department, but not the Program, and where the interviewer was ignorant of method of treatment and who recieved it.

In summary over the three points, then, there hardly seems any connection between the contents of the report and the statements of these reviewers.

Perhaps it should be pointed out in concluding this excursion into evaluative comments about "The Pre-Trail Intervention and Diversion Project" that final data are now available and analyses of these data are in process. Two reports that cover various phases of the analyses may be found in Binder and Palmer (1977) and Binder and Newkirk (forthcoming).

The objectivity associated with academic evaluators is pure fiction. They have personal biases, they have constituencies from which they derive status, and they have expectancies. Adams (1976:90) included academic (as well as journalistic) evaluators as "among our foremost obstacles to rationality in dealing with the problem of delinquency and crime"; and Brooks (1973) argued that academics are more interested in "career-boosting publications" than in serious program evaluation. Finally, Adams (1974) summarized Etzioni's arguments that academics tended to turn applied problems into basic research projects in their own interests.

Let me summarize by stating that in evaluating a social program, one determines if the new program is more cost-effective than a comparison program, or no program at all, where cost is broadly defined. The evaluation consists of a process that starts with goals and design, moves through data accumulation and analysis, and concludes with human interpretation. In formulating goals and comparing goals and outcomes, one must have a clear picture of the domain of evaluation—one is simply not determining the "effectiveness of diversion" when one, for example, introduces Transcendental Meditation to youngsters who are not petitioned at the level of probation; one is evaluating a specific process in a specific context. (In this context, note the important comments by Quay [forthcoming] in regard to the need for program integrity in the evaluation enterprise.) And evaluators of evaluations must clearly differentiate procedures and outcomes that show promise from those that repeatedly do not. The obtained empirical relationships may provide support for certain approaches, throw doubt on others, or even provide the first steps in developing an entirely different approach. In the final analysis, it is the evaluator who is the critical element. Thus, a set of evaluational results may convince one person of the usefulness of a given approach while another takes the position "Nothing works." Martinson (1976) and Palmer (1976), for example, look at the same data on the effectiveness of corrections and come out with interpretations of opposite directions. Unfortunately, the public as well as the political decision makers act on the reporter who makes the best press. I wish it were otherwise, but the academic reward system often reacts in a similar way.

As for the future, evaluation research must be oriented toward "what works for whom under what conditions" (Martinson and Wilks, 1976). It is clear that society will continue to designate many types of behavior as delinquent or criminal, even behavior that is only an aesthetic nuisance. It is clear, too, that delinquency and criminality have developmental components that are personally based in the array of ecological forces of which they are a part, and that these components become progressively more difficult to change as the developmental process advances. And, finally, it is clear that transient and "trivial" criminal-type behavior is a characteristic of virtually everybody—and when one gets caught in the justice net as a result of that trivial behavior, minimum or no treatment is most efficient for society and most effective for the individual.

Unless one argues that the justice system, supplemented by "no treatment," is the ultimate given to us by God, there is no question that we must continue to work at applying the knowledge of the behavioral and social sciences toward resolving difficulties that lead to these clashes with society. While pronouncements like "no treatment is sometimes better than treatment" and "diversion doesn't work" and "diversion is based upon the medical model" may lead to publications and personal advancements, they are of no help in advancing knowledge or practice. We must know the "what works," the "for whom," and the optimum conditions.

REFERENCES

ADAMS, S. (1974). "Evaluative research in corrections: Status and prospects." Federal Probation (March):14-21.

——— (1976). "Evaluation: A way out of rhetoric." Pp. 75-91 in Rehabilitation, recidivism, and research. Hackensack, N.J.: National Council on Crime and Delinquency.

ALEXANDER, J.F. and PARSONS, B.V. (1973). "Short term behavioral intervention with delinquent families: Impact on family process and recidivism." Journal of Abnormal Psychology, 81 (3):219-225.

BEVERIDGE, W.I.B. (1961). The art of scientific investigation. New York: Vintage Books.

BINDER, A. (1974). "Pre-trial intervention and diversion." Project no 1426, covering period September 1, 1973-August 31, 1974.

——— and Palmer, T.B. (1977). "A program in police diversion." Paper presented at the National Conference on Criminal Justice Evaluation, Washington, D.C., February.

BINDER, A. and NEWKIRK, M. (forthcoming) "A program to extend police service capability." Crime Prevention Review.

BROOKS, M. (1973). "Dimensions of and constraints on evaluative research." Proceedings of the Evaluation Symposium. Raleigh: North Carolina State Planning Agency, June.

CRESSEY, D.R. and McDERMOTT, R.A. (1973). Diversion from the juvenile justice system. National Assessment of Juvenile Corrections. Ann Arbor: University of Michigan.

DIXON, M.C. and WRIGHT, W.E. (1975). Juvenile delinquency prevention programs. An evaluations of policy related research on the effectiveness of prevention programs. Nashville, Tn.: Peabody College for Teachers, Office of Educational Services.

FISHMAN, R. (1975). "An evaluation of the effect on criminal recidivism of New York City projects providing rehabilitation and diversion services." Report to New York Criminal Justice Coordinating Council.

GEMIGNANI, R.J. (1972). "Youth services systems. Diverting youth from the juvenile justice system." Delinquency Prevention Reporter. Department of Health, Education and Welfare, Youth Development and Delinquency Prevention Administration, July-August.

GIBBONS, D.C. and BLAKE, G.F. (1976). "Evaluating the impact of juvenile diversion programs." Crime & Delinquency, 22(4):411-420.

HIGGINS, T. (1975). "Juvenile delinquency: Seeking effective prevention." Public Affairs Report, 16(6):1-7.

KITSUSE, J.I. (1962). "Societal reactions to deviant behavior: Problems of theory and method." Social Problems, 9(Winter):247-256.

KLAPMUTS, N. (1974). "Diversion from the justice system." Crime and Delinquency Literature, 6(March):108-131.

KLEIN, M.W. (1976a). "Issues in police diversion of juvenile offenders." Pp. 73-104 in R.M. Carter and M.W. KLEIN (eds.), Back on the street. The diversion of juvenile offenders. Englewood Cliffs, N.J.: Prentice-Hall.

———(1976b). "On the front end of the juvenile justice system." Pp. 307-313 in R.M. Carter and M.W. Klein (eds.), Back on the street. The diversion of juvenile offenders. Englewood Cliffs, N.J.: Prentice-Hall.

——— (1976c). "Issues and realities in police diversion programs." Crime & Delinquency, 22(4):421-427.

——— and TEILMANN, K.S. (1976). "Pivotal ingredients of police diversion programs." Project report submitted to National Institute for Juvenile Justice and Delinquency Prevention, U.S. Department of Justice.

KU, R. and BLEW, C.H. (1977). A university's approach to delinquency prevention. The adolescent diversion project. Urbana and Champaign, Illinois. An Exemplary Project. Washington, D.C.: U.S. Government Printing Office.

LEMERT, E.M. (1971). Instead of court: Diversion in juvenile justice. National Institute of Health Monograph Series: Crime and Delinquency issues. Washington, D.C.: U.S. Government Printing Office.

——— (1972). Human deviance, social problems, and social control. Englewood Cliffs, N.J.: Prentice-Hall.

LUNDMAN, R.J. (1976). "Will diversion reduce recidivism?" Crime & Delinquency, 22(4):428-437.

———, McFARLANE, P.T., and SCARPITTI, F.R. (1976). "Delinquency prevention. A description and assessment of projects reported in the professional literature." Crime & Delinquency, 22(3):297-308.

MARTINSON, R. (1976). "What works?—Questions and answers about prison reform." Pp. 7-39 in Rehabilition, recidivism, and research. Hackensack, N.J.: National Council on Crime and Delinquency.

——— and WILKS, J. (1976). Knowledge in criminal justice planning, a preliminary report. New York: The Center for Knowledge in Criminal Justice Planning.

PALMER, T. (1976). "Martinson revisted." Pp. 41-62 in Rehabilitation, recidivism, and research. Hackensack, N.J.: National Council on Crime and Delinquency.

PATTERSON, G.R., RAY, R.S., and SHAW, D.A. (1968). Direct intervention in families of deviant children. Oregon Research Institute Bulletin, 8(9).

President's Commission on Law Enforcement and Administration of Justice (1967). Challenge of crime in a free society. Washington, D.C.: U.S. Government Printing Office.

QUAY, H.C. (forthcoming). "The three faces of evaluation: What can be expected to work." Criminal Justice and Behavior.

RUTHERFORD, A. and McDERMOTT, R. (1976). Juvenile diversion. National Evaluation Program. Phase I Summary Report. U.S. Department of Justice, Law Enforcement Assistance Administration, National Institute of Law Enforcement and Criminal Justice.

SMITH, R. (1973). New Label—old practice." In P. Lejins (ed.), Criminal justice monographs: New approaches to diversion and treatment of juvenile offenders. Washington, D.C.: U.S. Government Printing Office.

TEILMANN, K.S., KLEIN, M.W., and STYLES, J.A. (1975). "The diversion explosion." Paper presented at the meeting of the Pacific Sociological Association, Victoria, B.C., April.

WEISS, C.H. (1972). Evaluation research. Methods for assessing program effectiveness. Englewood Cliffs, N.J.: Prentice-Hall.

ZIMRING, F.E. (1975). "Re: Robert Fishman, 'The effect on criminal recidivism of New York City projects providing rehabilitation and diversion services'." Mimeographed report from the University of Chicago, Center for Studies in Criminal Justice.

ABOUT THE AUTHORS

ROBERT H. ARONSON is Assistant Professor of Law at the University of Washington. Professor Aronson received his B.A. with Honors from the University of Virginia (1969), and his J.D. cum laude from the University of Pennsylvania (1973). He taught briefly at the University of San Diego and Stanford Law Schools before coming to the University of Washington Law School. He is a member of the Professional Responsibility sections of the American Bar Association, Association of American Law Schools, and Society of American Law Teachers.

ARNOLD BINDER is a Professor in the Program in Social Ecology, University of California, Irvine, a program that he conceived in 1968 and launched as an academic unit in 1970. He is currently an associate editor of the *Journal of Criminal Justice* and director of an exploratory police diversion project. The diversion project, supported by major LEAA funding, is based upon contractual arrangements between the University of California and 14 separate police departments.

CAROL BOHMER obtained her B.A. and LL. M. degree from Victoria University of Wellington, New Zealand, a post graduate diploma in Criminology from Cambridge University, and a Ph.D. from the University of Pennsylvania. She has been involved in sociolegal research with sex offenders, rape victims, comparative matrimonial law, and the use of psychiatric evidence in the criminal law. She is presently Associate Professor at Rutgers Law School, Camden, New Jersey.

ALVIN W. COHN currently is Technical Director for the Executive Training Program in Advanced Criminal Justice Practices and Senior Associate with University Research Corporation. He is the founder and president of his own consulting firm, Administration of Justice Services, in Rockville, Maryland, and formerly was on the full- and part-time faculties of American University, Virginia Commonwealth University, George Washington University, and the University of Southern California—Washington Public Affairs Center. He has been the Director of the Proba-Management Institutes and Director of Training for the National Council on Crime and Delinquency and has worked in adult and juvenile probation, parole, and institutional settings. He is the author or coauthor of five books and numerous professional articles. He is also the coeditor of *The Criminologist,* the official newsletter of the American Society of Criminology. He holds an A.B. in sociology from the University of Cincinnati, an M.A. in psychiatric social work from Indiana University, and a Doctorate in Criminology from the University of California, Berkeley.

SUSAN G. DALTON is currently a Research Assistant in the Division of Addiction Sciences in the Department of Psychiatry—University of Miami School of Medicine. Since receiving her B.A. degree from the University of Tennessee, she has been involved in research on cultural health care practices in various ethnic groups, the effect of adolescents' relationships with parents and peers on their drug use patterns, and the effectiveness of criminal justice diversion for drug users.

RICHARD FOSTER is currently an Assistant Professor of Government at Idaho State University specializing in planning and public administration. He received his Ph.D. and Master's of Public Administration from the University of Oklahoma.

MICHAEL S. KATZ is the Executive Director of the Criminal Justice Planning Committee of Washoe County (Reno), Nevada. He has several publications in various fields of criminal justice, has worked as a local police officer, taught classes at the community college, and lectured at the University of Nevada. He is in the process of completing the thesis requirement for his M.A. in Sociology, with a field of concentration in criminology.

MARLYNN L. MAY, Ph.D., teaches sociology at Beloit College, Beloit, Wisconsin, specializing in deviance, criminal justice, and social philosophy. Simultaneously, since 1971, he has been a staff member of Rock Valley (Wisconsin) Community Corrections, Inc., as the Director of Evaluation Research and Planning. He is presently writing an extensive critique of evaluation research, evaluating its failures and promises in the field of criminal justice.

DUANE C. McBRIDE is currently an Assistant Professor in the Department of Psychiatry—University of Miami School of Medicine and serves as Deputy Director of the Department's Division of Addiction Sciences. He received his M.A. from the University of Maryland in 1970 and his Ph.D. from the University of Kentucky in 1976. Since 1973 he has been conducting research on the effectiveness of treatment services for drug users with a particular emphasis on the linkage between drug users in the criminal justice system and community drug treatment programs. He is also author of numerous articles in professional journals.

ROBERT M. REGOLI is an Assistant Professor of Sociology at Texas Christian University. He received his Ph.D. in Sociology from Washington State University (1975). Since then, he has published numerous articles in the professional journals and is the author of *Police In America* (1976). Presently, he is working on several police related research projects with the results to be forthcoming in the near future.

RONALD SCHNEIDER is presently an Assistant Professor of Criminal Justice at Florida International University. He received his Ph.D. and Master's degrees from the University of Southern California.

SAGE RESEARCH PROGRESS SERIES IN CRIMINOLOGY

Series Editors: GILBERT GEIS and JAMES A. INCIARDI

Published in cooperation with the American Society of Criminology, this series of concisely edited works presents notable, previously unpublished writing on topics of current concern to the international community of criminologists. The original essays selected for publication in each volume of this series have a topicality and scope that makes them ideal for the instructor of criminology, as well as the researcher and practitioner.

...NS
...essional Social Science
...y Hills London